D1725514

System Administration (SAP HANA as a Database) with SAP NetWeaver

SAP Certified Technology Associate

By

B Landry & S Kaur

Copyright Notice

Contents

Before you Start..

Before you start here are some Key features of the **SAP Certified Technology Associate – System Administration (SAP HANA as a Database) with SAP NetWeaver** Certification Exam.

- ✓ This certification path will **validate** your capability as a well-trained associate prepared to help your client or employer manage and execute key business processes.

- ✓ Associate Certifications are targeting profiles with **1 - 5 years** of knowledge and experience. The primary source of knowledge and skills is based on the corresponding training material.

- ✓ The exam is **Computer based** and you have three Hours to answer 80 Questions.

- ✓ The Questions are (mostly) **multiple choice** type and there is NO penalty for an incorrect answer.

- ✓ Some of the Questions have more than one correct answer. You must get **ALL** the options correct for you to be awarded points.

- ✓ For questions with a single answer, the answers will have a button next to them. You will be able to select only one button.

- ✓ For questions with multiple answers, the answers will have a 'tick box' next to them. This allows you to select multiple answers.

- ✓ You are **not** allowed to use any reference materials during the certification test (no access to online documentation or to any SAP system).

- ✓ The Official Pass percentage is **63%. (This can vary slightly for your exam)**

- ✓ In this book, unless otherwise stated, there is only one correct answer.

Installation (AS ABAP and AS JAVA)

1. **Which of the following port is used by SAPinst to communicate with the GUI server?**

   a. 21212
   b. 21200
   c. 21201
   d. 4239

Answer: b

Explanation:

Communication Ports Used During SAP System Installation
During installation the default ports 21200, 21212 and 4239 are used for communication between SAPinst, GUI server, SAPinst GUI, and HTTP server.

Default Communication Ports
- SAPinst communicates with the GUI server through port 21200.
- The GUI server communicates with SAPinst GUI through port 21212.
- The HTTP server port is 4239, which is a part of the GUI server.

You receive an error notification if one of these ports is already in use by another service. In this case, start SAPinst with the command line parameters.

SAPinst Command Line Parameters
- SAPINST_DIALOG_PORT=<free_port_nurmber_sapinst_gui_to_gui_server>
- GUISERVER_DIALOG_PORT=<free_port_number_gui_server_to_sapinst_gui>
- GUISERVER_HTTP_PORT-<free_port_number_http_server>

2. **Which of the following are the key principles of Landscape Virtualization Management?**

   Note: There are two correct answers to the question

   a. Adaptive
   b. Simplified
   c. Coherent
   d. Unified

Answer: b, d

Explanation:

SAP Landscape Virtualization Management provides a central point of control for flexibly assigning computing hosts and managing application instances in the system landscape. SAP

Landscape Virtualization Management is built on four key principles:

- **Unified** - Reduce the time and effort to transition to virtual and cloud environments by decoupling the application from the underlying infrastructure; by providing a unified view and management of the hardware, software, and virtualization layers; and by automating system relocation.
- **Complete** - Improve your ability to respond to business needs with support for configuring, deploying, monitoring, and managing your SAP systems and landscapes in both physical and virtualized infrastructures providing you more infrastructure options and faster time to value.
- **Simplified** - Simplify the management of SAP landscapes by hiding the technical complexities of physical and virtualized infrastructures from day-to-day operations.
- **Automated** - Reduce the capital investment and operational costs (that is TCO) of your SAP systems by scheduling system operations in advance with a built-in task planner; and leveraging virtualization to reduce your hardware requirements and improve host utilization.

3. **Which of the following file records the notifications of every installation step?**

   a. Sapinst.log
   b. Keydb.xml
   c. Sapinst_dev.log
   d. Packages.xml

Answer: c

Explanation:

Primary SAPinst Log Files

Sapinst.log: Information on the installation progress
Sapinst_dev.log: Records in detail all of the notifications of every installation step.

You can find the log files sapinst.log and sapinst_dev.log in the current installation directory. Additional log files may be written during the installation process. The additional logs are referenced in sapinst.log and sapinst_dev.log

Location of SAPinst GUI and the GUI Server Log Files

- Windows: %userprofile%\.stdgui
- UNIX: <user_home>/.stdgui

If SAPinst GUI does not start check the sdtstart.err file in the current %userprofile% (Windows) or <user_home> (UNIX) directory.

4. **Which of the following Windows specific preparations are performed when installing an SAP system on a Windows Operating system?**

   Note: There are two correct answers to the question

a. Check windows File system
b. Prepare Installation User
c. Check System Registry
d. Change the program files directory permissions

Answer: a, b

Explanation:

Windows File System NTFS
You can install an SAP system on Windows only on NTFS-formatted partitions. Set the paging file size according to the recommendations of the installation guides and the Prerequisite Check tool. SAPinst generates a prompt asking if you would like to adapt page settings.

Domain or Local Installation
You can decide whether you want to install your system on the hosts locally or using a Windows domain. It is recommended to install your system using a domain. For a domain installation, it is recommended that all SAP systems and database hosts are members of a single Windows domain.
This recommendation is valid for all SAP system setups, whether standalone central systems or distributed systems. In the single Windows domain model, the SAP system and the user accounts are included in a single Windows domain.

5. Which of the following SAP file systems need to be setup manually for installations on UNIX operating systems?

   Note: There are two correct answers to the question

   a. SCS<No>
   b. ASCS<No>
   c. /<sapmnt>
   d. /usr/sap

Answer: c, d

Explanation:

During the installation process, set up the file systems and raw devices for the SAP system and database. Manually set up the file systems as shown in the previous figure. SAPinst does the rest of the set up during the installation process. If you do not set up any file system on your installation host SAPinst creates all directories in the root directory (/).

SAPinst prompts you only for directory <sapmnt> during the installation. The file system starting from SCS<No> is from the Central Services instance of an Application Server (AS) Java or AS ABAP and Java system. Only file system ASCS<No> is relevant to a high availability (HA) installation of an AS ABAP or AS ABAP and Java system.

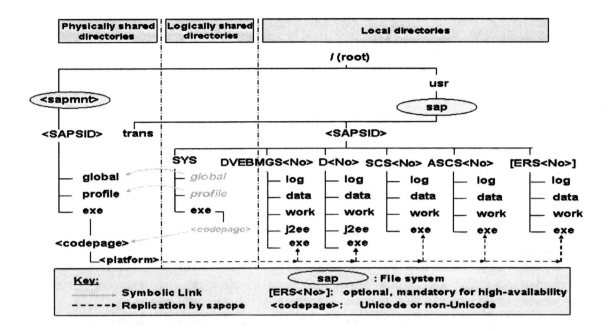

Note: For systems based on SAP Net Weaver AS 7.10 and later the kernel file system structure for UNIX is adjusted so that it is the same as for Windows. This means that ... /SYS/exe/<codepage>/<platform> folder replaces ... / SYS/ exe /run folder where <codepage> stands for nuc or uc, depending on whether it is a non-Unicode or Unicode kernel. Here <platform> specifies the operating system platform, for example, linuxx86_64.

6. Which of the following rules apply to the SAP System ID?

   Note: There are three correct answers to the question

   a. The SAP System ID must be unique
   b. The SAP System ID must consists of three alphanumeric characters
   c. The SAP System ID must consists of only lowercase characters
   d. The first character must be a letter and subsequent characters may be digits
   e. The first character must be a special character and subsequent character may be digits

Answer: a, c, d

Explanation:

Rules Concerning the SAP System ID

The SAP system ID must conform to specific naming conventions.
SAP system ID (<SID>) Naming Conventions

- The SAP system ID (<SAPSID> or <SID>) and database system ID (<DBSID>) must be unique.
- The SAP system ID must consist of three alphanumeric characters.
- Only uppercase letters are allowed.
- The first character must be a letter and the subsequent characters may be digits.

7. **Which of the following type of data stored in the SAP Databases?**

    a. Master data
    b. Transaction Data
    c. Logging Data
    d. All of the above

Answer: d

Explanation:

Type of Data Stored in SAP Databases
- Business data (master data. transaction data. and so on) and the corresponding index data
- Logging data for the database (needed for recovery)

Databases of SAP systems are usually stored on disks combined with some Redundant Array of Inexpensive Disks (RAID) level (usually 1or5) or on Storage Area Networks (SANs).

Databases used for SAP systems can hold up to several terabytes of business data because practically you are unable to restore a large database and you have to ensure that data loss is avoided under almost all circumstances. The disk layout for databases used for SAP systems affects not only the performance of SAP systems but also their reliability and availability.

8. **How do you specify the SAP system for which you would like install an AAS?**

    a. The AAS is automatically installed for the <SID> of the <SID>adm user you are using to execute the installation
    b. When using SAPinst you are prompted for the profile directory of the system for which you would like to install an AAS
    c. You need to start SAPinst from the SYS directory of the system for which you would like to install an AAS
    d. AAS installation is possible only from the host where the Gateway instance is installed

Answer: b

Explanation:

In an AS ASAP-based system, all AASs are installed as AS ABAP instances. Similarly, in an AS Java-based SAP system, all AASs are installed as AS Java instances and in an AS ASAP and AS Java-based SAP system; all AASs are installed as AS ABAP and Java instances.

The installation procedure is the same in all three cases. The procedure only differs in the number of phases and the time needed for installation. An AS ASAP-based dialog instance can be installed in a few minutes, provided the server does not host too many additional SAP systems or instances - then the setting of the Access Control List might take a long time (because many files in \usr\sap need to be touched and their access rights must be checked).

Enter the profile directory of the SAP ECC system you installed as shown below.

9. **In which of the following phase you can revise the parameters value during the SAP solution manager system installation?**

    a. Parameter Summary
    b. Execution
    c. Initial Phase
    d. Define Parameters

Answer: a

Explanation:

The Parameter Summary screen allows you to review all parameters set so far. If you want to change a specific setting, you can check the box next to it and choose *Revise* from the bottom line options. If you do not mark at least one of the input parameter the *Revise* button remains gray. To start the dialog-free part of the installation, choose next.

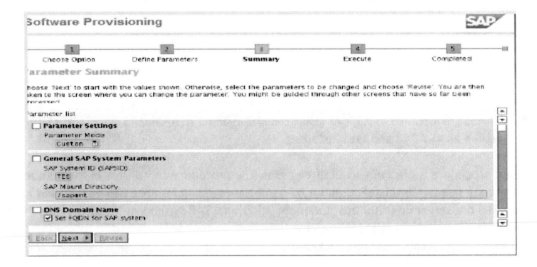

10. **Which of the following options are the two major steps to install SAP Online documentation?**

   Note: There are two correct answers to the question

   a. Install the help files
   b. Change the message server host
   c. Customize setup variants for online help
   d. Rename your SAP system ID

Answer: a, c

Explanation:

Steps to Install SAP Net Weaver Online Help

1. Create a folder for the installation, for example, D:\documentation.
2. Start *sapinst.exe* from the installation master DVD.
3. In SAPinst provide the language folder on the documentation DVD.
4. Wait until the installation completes and close SAPinst.
5. To open the SAP Library, choose *<local folder>\HTMLHELP\<Language>\00000001.chm*.

PlainHtmlHttp and PlainHtmlfile Help Installation

The standard HTML files for PlainHtmlHttp and PlainHtmlfile help types are stored in a packed format in the archive Plainhtm.sar on the DVD. They cannot be viewed directly from the DVD and must be unpacked on a file server before they can be used. To unpack the help files, you must use SAPinst which is included on the installation master DVD.

The complete installation comprises nearly 400,000 files in 200,000 directories for one language version. Depending on the file system and the configuration of the hard disk about 3 GB of disk space is required.

You cannot install online help on a Microsoft FAT32 file system because it cannot process such large numbers of files and directories. If your web server runs on Microsoft Windows, choose another partition and do not install the help documentation on the system partition.

11. **Which of the following are the benefits of SAP Router?**

   Note: There are three correct answers to the question

   a. Increases network security
   b. Determines the language version of the online help displays
   c. Offers its customers access to support
   d. Required for remote support connections
   e. Simplifies Network configuration

Answer: a, d, e

Explanation:

- SAP router increases network security simplifies network configuration and allows you to make indirect network connections. SAP router is required for remote support connections.
- SAP router Functions Controls and logs connections to your SAP system, for example, from an SAP service center
- Sets up indirect connection when programs involved in the connection cannot communicate with each other due to the network configuration
- Improves network security by means of:
    - ✓ A password, which helps to protect your connection and data from unauthorized external access
    - ✓ Access from particular SAP routers only
    - ✓ Access of only encrypted connect ions from a known partner by using the Secure Network Communication (SNC) layer
- Increases performance and stability by reducing the SAP system workload in a LAN when communicating with a WAN

12. **Which of the following steps are needed to install additional languages?**

    Note: There are three correct answers to the question

    a. Classifying the language
    b. Scheduling of language transport or import
    c. Scheduling of language supplementation
    d. Supplementing of periodic language for newly generated texts
    e. Regenerating the language texts for translation

Answer: a, b, c

Explanation:

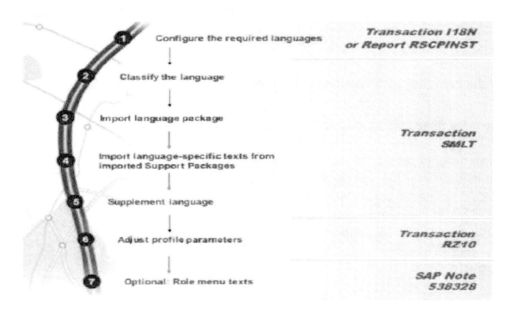

We need to classify the language, schedule language transport or import and schedule language supplementation to install additional languages.

Depending on the release status the SAP system supports up to 40 different languages. The language with which a user works is specified through entry on the logon screen by a system default or by a default set ting in the user master record.

This language must first be imported into the SAP system before users can log on with the desired language. Only German (DE) and English (EN) are initially installed after a new installation of an SAP system. If required you can use transaction SMLT to import additional languages.

If you select a language (other than DE, EN, or Japanese) you should note that the selected language is not fully translated. The texts that are not translated in the selected language must be provided using a supplemental language. This supplement al language must be a completely translated language. This can also be recursively configured so that you use a number of supplemental languages.

13. **Which protocol is used to implement the cross system standard scenarios?**

    a. Transmission control Protocol
    b. Remote Function Call
    c. Internet Protocol
    d. SAP Mail Transfer Protocol

Answer: b

Explanation:

When using standard cross-system SAP processes such as an SAP ERP Central Component system connected to an external system that is for example not RFC-enabled it is useful to install a standalone SAP Gateway instance.

These cross-system standard scenarios are implemented through Remote Function Call (RFC).For example, for Human Resource (HR) reasons, (such as time registration), you use third-party software to read the access cards of the employees entering or leaving the company. This information needs to be transferred to your SAP ERP Central Component (HR) system to be processed.

It the time registration software is not RFC enabled, you can install a standalone SAP Gateway instance on the host of the third-party software. The time registration software can communicate with the SAP Gateway instance, for example, through Transmission Control Protocol (TCP) or Internet Protocol (IP).

Within your SAP ERP Central Component system you can use the standard RFC-based scenarios to communicate through the standalone SAP Gateway with the time registration software.

14. **Which of the following are the advantages of SAPinst compared to R3setup?**

    Note: There are two correct answers to the question

a. Set back to correct your entries during the input phase without restarting the installation
b. It does not abort because of errors occurred during the installation
c. It records installation progress in a multiple log file
d. You cannot start SAPinst GUI on a remote server

Answer: a, c

Explanation:

The System Landscape Implementation Manager (SAPinst) offers these main advantages compared to R3SETUP:

- SAPinst lets you step back to correct your entries during the input phase without restarting the installation.

- SAPinst does not abort because of errors. Instead, it stops the installation and you can retry the installation after solving the problem. Alternatively, you can abort the installation manually if you want.

- SAPinst continues an aborted installation directly from the point of failure.

- SAPinst records installation progress in a single log file, **sapinst.log**.

- You can start SAPinst GUI on a remote computer if you want.

- SAPinst has a graphical user interface (GUI), SAPinst GUI, which allows you to monitor the progress of the installation and see all messages issued by SAPinst

15. **An SAP System must be installed on which file system of Windows?**

    a. FAT
    b. HPFS
    c. NTFS
    d. None of the above

Answer: c

Explanation:

An SAP system must be installed on an NTFS file system.

NTFS (New Technology File System) is the standard file system of Windows NT, including its later versions Windows 2000, Windows XP, Windows Server 2003, Windows Server 2008,Windows Vista, and Windows 7.

Do not install the SAP directories on a FAT partition. Check the partition on which you plan to install the SAP system for the correct file system.

Follow this procedure to check the file system of the installation partition:
- Open Windows Explorer.
- Select the root directory.
- Choose Properties.
- Switch to the General tab to see the type of file system that is in use

16. **Which of the following preparations are required before installing or run the SAPinst in the context of Windows?**

    a.   Java Software Development Kit to be installed
    b.   Clean up the JDK\ext directory
    c.   Set the JAVA_HOME environment variable
    d.   All of the above

Answer: d

Explanation:

SAPinst is a Java-based tool, the Java Software Development Kit (abbreviated as SDK or JDK) must be installed on all hosts where SAPinst will run. After installing the Java SDK, some rework is mandatory.

Check the Java \ext directory to see if there is already <parser_name>.jar files. If exist, rename them for the current installation. Remember to rename the files back to their original names after the installation procedure is complete. SAPinst needs the JAVA_HOME environment variable to be set on the host(s) where SAPinst will run. Check if the system variable JAVA_HOME is set to the Java home directory; if it is not set create a new variable.

You have to add the Java home directory to the Path variable. Enter **%JAVA_HOME%\bin** at the end of the Variable Value field. Use a semicolon (;) to separate the entry from the previous entry!

17. **Which of the following value to be set for the DISPLAY environment variable to run the SAPinst in the context of UNIX?**

    a.   <host_name>0.0
    b.   <host_name>1.0
    c.   <host_name>2.0
    d.   None of the above

Answer: a

Explanation:

Make sure that DISPLAY is set to <hostname>:0.0, where<hostname> is the host on which SAPinst GUI is to be displayed. Typically, this is the hostname or IP address of your local host.

18. **Which of the following statement is true for Unicode SAP system installation in the context of UNIX?**

a. The setting of the library path environment variable is required only for the central system and the database instance installation
b. The setting of the library path environment variable is does not required
c. The setting of the library path environment variable is required only specific instances
d. The setting of the library path environment variable is required for all SAP instance installations

Answer: d

Explanation:

Non-Unicode SAP system installation:
- The setting of the library path environment variable is required only for the central system and the database instance installation.
Unicode SAP system installation:
- The setting of the library path environment variable is required for all SAP instance installations.

19. SAPinst first checks the availability and location of the required installation CDs or Software packages during the installation process. Which file contains the information about these software packages or installation CDs?

    a. dialog.xml
    b. Message.asc
    c. Label.asc
    d. None of the above

Answer: c

Explanation:

SAPinst first checks the and finally verify the availability and location of the required installation CDs or Software packages. The information of these CDs or Packages is stored in a file called LABEL.ASC.

During the Installation process, System displays a CD browser which takes the location of the file LABEL.ASC in the "PACKAGE LOCATION" column and also ticks the check box "CHECK LOCATION".

20. If you want to install one SAP system from another SAP system having the same database system and operating system, which installation method can be used to copy the SAP system?

    a. Homogeneous System copy
    b. Heterogeneous System copy
    c. Migration System copy
    d. All of the above

Answer: a

Explanation:

- You perform a homogeneous system copy if your target system is on the same operating system and database system as your source system. The database contents are copied from the source system to the target system.
- You perform a heterogeneous system copy if you want to change the operating system or database system. Migration is another term for a heterogeneous system copy.

When you perform a system copy, all software units or usage types in the source system are copied to the target system. This means that none of the usage types in the target system can be excluded from the system copy, nor can you select usage types.

21. **Which of the following user is required to enable communication between ABAP and JAVA stack?**

    a. SAPUSER
    b. SAPJSF
    c. SAPJER
    d. None of the above

Answer: b

Explanation:

The user SAPJSF is required to enable communication between ABAP and Java stack. User SAPJSF will be created using the function module.

The communication user SAPJSF is used during the user authentication that takes place between the JEEE Security service and the SAP Web Application Server by RFC communication.
During the installation of the SAP Web Application Server and/or the activation of the J2EE Engine, the communication user is automatically created and received the role SAP_BC_JSF_COMMUNICATION_RO.

This means that the user has only read access to all user data and can. The role contains the authorization with which the communications user can authenticate the end user. During the installation or activation of the SAP J2EE Engine, the system prompts you to specify a password for the communication user. The communication user is then automatically created.

22. **If the dialog instance is installed on the same host as the central instance, which of the following statement is correct?**

    a. Both instances must be assigned to same number
    b. Both instances must be assigned to different numbers
    c. No number assignment is required
    d. All of the above

Answer: b

Explanation:

If more than one instance running on the same host, both instances must be assigned different numbers. So, if you are installing dialog instance on the same host as the central instance, you must assign different numbers. You can specify a value from 00 to 97.

23. **Which of the following is the default message server port number in the central instance installation?**

   a. 30<Instance Number>
   b. 35<Instance Number>
   c. 36<Instance Number>
   d. 33<Instance Number>

Answer: c

Explanation:

The default message server port number in the central instance installation is 36<Instance Number>.
Instance number is the same number given for the central instance.
Instance Number is the two digit number given at the time of installation.
The port number of the message server port must be the same as the one on the central instance host

System Administration (AS ABAP and AS Java)

24. Which of the following work process types are there in the SAP System?

Note: There are three correct answers to the question

    a.   Update Work process
    b.   Spool Work Process
    c.   Instance Work Process
    d.   Dialog work process
    e.   Gateway work Process

Answer: a, b, d

Explanation:

The ICM (Internet Communication Manager) is not a work process but a service of the SAP Net Weaver Application Server; similarly, the gateway. The instance itself is not a work process. In addition to the correct work process types listed above, there are also background work processes and Enqueue work processes.

- Dialog work processes (**D**) deal with requests from an active user to execute dialog steps. Each dispatcher needs at least two dialog work processes.
- The Update work processes (**U or V**) execute database update requests. Update requests are part of an SAP LUW that bundle the database operations resulting from the dialog in a database LUW for processing in the background. It is possible to configure more than one per dispatcher.
- The Enqueue work process (**E**) administers a lock table in the shared memory area. The lock table contains the logical database locks for Net Weaver AS ABAP and is an important part of the SAP LUW concept. In NW AS, you may only have one lock table. You may therefore also only have one ABAP application server with Enqueue work processes. Normally, a single Enqueue work process is sufficient to perform the required tasks.
- Background work processes process (**B**) programs that can be executed without user interaction (background jobs). Each SAP system needs at least two background work processes. You can configure more than one background work process per dispatcher.
- The spool work process (**S**) passes sequential datasets to a printer or to optical archiving. Each ABAP SAP System contains at least one spool work process. It is possible to configure more than one spool work process per dispatcher

25. Which of the following technology ABAP based SAP systems use to process user requests?

    a.   Work process Multiplexing
    b.   Dispatcher handling
    c.   VM container technology
    d.   Communication Manager

Answer: a

Explanation:

Dialog Work Process Multiplexing: The processing of a transaction that consists of multiple screens is usually executed using multiple, different dialog work processes. This distribution is called work process multiplexing. Work process multiplexing means that a system function whose content is logically connected but consists of multiple sub steps can be processed by various dialog work processes.

These steps, where the content is connected, are described as transactions. A transaction that consists of multiple screens, such as screens 100 and 200 can also be processed by multiple dialog work processes.

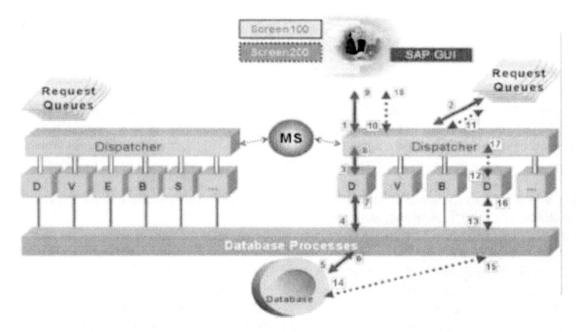

The figure shows two screens of a transaction (100 and 200), for which the input is handled by two different dialog work processes. The multiplexing procedure is used exclusively for dialog work processes. All other work process types process entire functions; that is, complete business processes.

As dialog work processes may therefore process only parts of transactions that are connected from a business point of view; the update procedure with the update work process is widely used in SAP systems.

26. **Which of the following work mode helps you to inform users on planned downtime and maintenance windows?**

     a. Business Work Mode
     b. Transactional Work Mode
     c. Technical Work Mode
     d. Analytical work Mode

Answer: c

Explanation:

Within SAP Solution Manager you can use work modes to plan, notify, and execute work modes for technical systems, databases, technical scenarios, instances and logon groups.

On the one hand Work Mode Management is used to define **Business Work Modes**, which helps you to adapt the monitoring thresholds of the involved systems to the current system load.

On the other hand, you can use **Technical Work Modes**. This helps you to inform users of planned downtime and maintenance windows for activities like:

- Patch upgrades
- Upgrades
- Database, hardware, or operating system maintenance
- Configuration or customizing changes
- Migration

27. **In which of the following profile you can change the number of background work process?**

     a. Start profile
     b. Default profile
     c. Background profile
     d. Instance profile

Answer: d

Explanation:

- The instance profile is the correct profile as settings in this profile only apply to the affected instance, and the number of work processes for an instance is defined here.
- The start profile contains information about the processes to be started during the system start. In the default profile, you maintain parameters that apply to all instances or for the entire SAP system.
- The background profile does not exist in SAP system.

28. **Which of the following is the correct sequence of setting up operation modes?**
     1. **Create Operation Mode**
     2. **Distribute work process**
     3. **Maintain Time table**
     4. **Assign instances**

     a. 1,2,3,4
     b. 1,4,2,3
     c. 1,3,2,4
     d. 1,3,4,2

Answer: b

Explanation:

Create operation modes using transaction RZ04 to perform the following steps.

Create two operation modes, Day and Night:

- You can maintain operation modes in transaction RZ04 (Tools →CCMS → Configuration → Operation Modes/Instances).
- You can create operation modes by choosing the Create operation mode (F5) pushbutton. Enter the name of the operation mode and a short description and choose Save. Repeat the procedure for the second operating mode.
- When you have finished, you should see two operation modes in the input screen CCMS: Maintain Operation Modes and Instances.

Create a definition for the work process distribution for all instances of your system:

- Switch to the Instances/Operation Modes view by choosing the *Instances/operation modes (F6)* pushbutton. This is identified by the line *Productive instances and their WP distribution*.
- You define work process distribution for all instances of your system by choosing *Settings → Based on current status → new instances →Generate*.
- Result: Two additional lines appear at the end of the input screen. Activate your entries by choosing the *Save* pushbutton.

Change the distribution of the work processes of your instances for each of the operation modes:

- Note that there should be at least two dialog and two background work processes in all operation modes.
- To change the distribution of the work processes for the operation modes of the instances, double click the operation modes entries. Start with the operation mode Day. You change and then save the distribution of the work processes in the dialog box: CCMS: Maintain Work Process Distribution.
- To do this, place the cursor in the column of the work process type that you want to change. You can change the number by choosing + and -.
- Do not forget to change the operation mode Night as well. The easiest way to do this is by using the pushbutton other operation mode. To the right of the field for Operation Mode, press F4 to select the operation mode Night. Then save the work process distribution for both operation modes by choosing save.

After you have changed the distribution for all operation modes and instances, choose the Save pushbutton in the input screen CCMS: Maintain Operation Modes and Instances in the system function bar.

29. Which of the following are the reasons for the data archiving?

- a. Improved response times
- b. Cost reduction
- c. System downtime reduces

    d. All of the above

Answer: d

Explanation:

The larger a database is, the higher the cost for database administration with regard to recovery or backup. Securing the SAP system services requires ever more resources. Upgrades of the system or database also become disproportionately more expensive with an increasing database size.

For end users, an increasing database size means a higher system load for individual database queries; that is, increasing response times for reporting and access to individual database records

The reasons for data archiving are summarized in the following list:

- Improve response times or ensure good response times
- Reduce costs for database administration
- Reduce system downtime for software upgrades, recoveries, and (offline) data backups
- Legal requirements and business requirements must be taken into account here, such as:
    - ✓ Country-specific retention rules
    - ✓ Data must be available to auditors
    - ✓ Potential reusability of data

Data must be archived in a way that they can be called at any time for queries. These queries could, for example, be from tax authorities. There are legal data retention requirements in each country. Also, only data from completed business processes can be archived.

With data archiving, data is archived independent of the hardware and software release statuses (metadata is stored). In this way, it is still possible to call archived data without any problems even after a system upgrade.

30. Which of the following are the different options available for testing a RFC destination?

    a. Connection Test
    b. Authorization Test
    c. Unicode Test
    d. All of the above

Answer: d

Explanation:

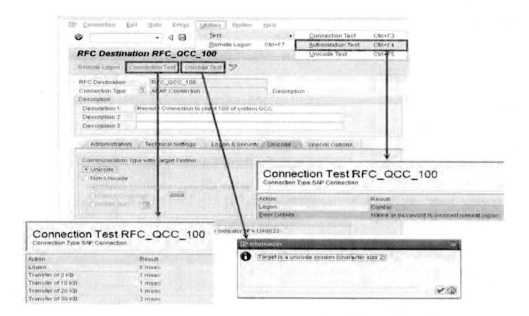

You have three options for testing a destination:

- You can attempt to log on to the remote system. To do this, choose Remote Login. A new session opens for the remote system. Enter the client, your user name, and your password. If you have stored a dialog user with password in the connection, a dialog logon is performed .If you have defined a communication user or system user, you can check that the specified password is correct under Utilities → Test → Authorization Test.

- With a connection test (Test Connection button or the menu path Utilities → Test → Connection Test), the system tries to establish a "technical" connection with the target system and then displays a table with response times. If an error message appears, check your settings. This test is a pure "technical" connection test, and only checks whether a partner system can be reached with the specifications you have made.

- During the Unicode test (Button Unicode test or Utilities → Test →Unicode Test, the system checks the "Unicodeness" of the remote SAP system and shows the result of this check.

31. Which of the following access methods exist in the SAP system?

    Note: There are three correct answers to the question

    a. Remote Printing
    b. Front-end Printing
    c. Instance Printing
    d. Local Printing
    e. Laser Printing

Answer: a, b, d

Explanation:

Local Printing: In local printing, the spool work process and operating system spool run on the same host. It is irrelevant whether the printer is directly connected to this host, or is reached over a network (and possibly another print server). The spool work process passes on its data locally that is on the same host.

Remote Printing: With remote printing, the spool work process and operating system spooler run on different hosts. In the same way as with local printing, it is irrelevant from the SAP system's point of view whether the printer is directly connected to the remote host, or is reached using a network connection.

Front-end Printing: SAP users can output documents on their local printers using front-end printing. These local printers do not need to be individually defined in the SAP system. Rather the system administrator only needs to create a representative output device for each operating system platform.

32. **Which of the following listed states can a spool request have?**

   Note: There are three correct answers to the question

   a. Complete
   b. Canceled
   c. Error
   d. Waiting
   e. Active

Answer: a, c, d

Explanation:

Transaction SP01 provides many **selection criteria** for selecting particular spooler output requests. The 'Further selection criteria' function is simple to use and allows each user to define their own selection criteria.
The displayed list shows all spool or output requests that match your selection criteria. The list is created using the SAP List Viewer (ALV). This allows you to change the appearance of the list as you desire. This means that you can show and hide columns, sort columns, or create variants.

The following indicators specify the **status** of a spool request:

-
Not yet sent to the operating system (no output request exists).
+
Spool request is just being created (stored in spool system).
Waiting
The output request has not yet been processed by the spool system.
Waiting in host spooler
The output request is to be sent or is being sent to the spool work process, or for formatting, in the host spool system.

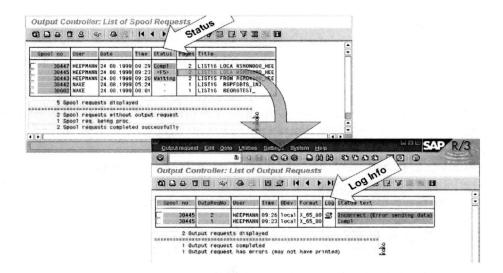

Processing
A spool work process is formatting the output request for printing.
Printing
The request has been passed to the host spooler or to an output device, and a final status has not yet been returned to the SAP spool system.
Complete
The output request has been printed. If the query at the host spooler is not activated, the status changes to Completed as soon as the output request is transferred to the host spooler.
<F5>
There are (at least two) output requests with various statuses.
Problem
Indicates an error not of a serious nature (such as incomplete character set) this request was still printed.
Error
Indicates a serious error such as a network error
Time
A particular time was specified for the output of the request by the request creator.
Archive
The spool request has been processed by the spool system and is waiting to be archived (for spool requests sent to an archiving device).

33. **Which of the following access method is used for External Output Management Systems?**

   a.   Access Method L
   b.   Access Method G
   c.   Access Method E
   d.   Access Method M

Answer: c

Explanation:

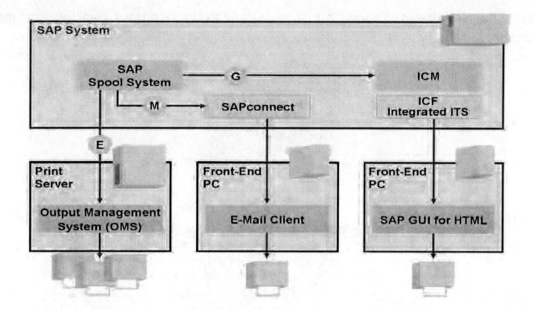

External Output Management Systems (OMS) can be addressed from the SAP system using a defined interface (BC-XOM) (access method E). This method is of particular interest if you have a very large volume, or the output of multiple systems (SAP systems and others) is to be centrally controlled and monitored.

In addition, you can **send print output by e-mail** to a user (access method M). The e-mail is sent using SAP connect. A user can also be connected to an SAP system from a web browser using SAP GUI for HTML. This type of connection can be set up in the SAP system with the integrated ITS as of AS ABAP 6.40

34. In which of the following criteria SAP recommends to use Printing Assistant for Landscapes (PAL)?

    a. Several output devices in a few SAP systems
    b. A Few output device in several SAP systems
    c. Several output devices in several SAP systems
    d. All of the above

Answer: d

Explanation:

Printing Assistant for Landscapes can be used to simplify the administration of output devices in ABAP-based SAP systems. To do this, output devices are maintained in one system (normally the central system), and their definition is then distributed across any number of additional systems (target systems) over RFC.

SAP recommends using PAL if at least one of the following criteria applies:

- You manage several output devices in a few SAP systems.
- You manage a few output devices in several SAP systems.
- You manage several output devices in several SAP systems.

The following diagram is based on a small PAL landscape, and shows the release requirements of the systems involved:

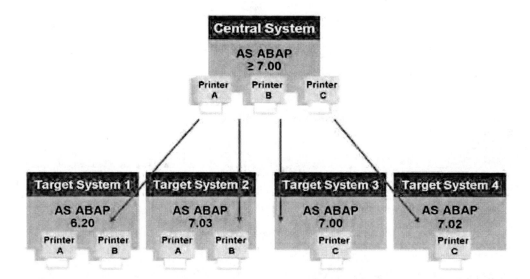

The central system must be based on an AS ABAP 7.00 (or higher) with an up-to-date patch level. Since the SAP Solution Manager system also supports you to manage other functions centrally, you can use and SAP Solution Manager 7.1 system as the central system for PAL. The target systems must have a minimum release level of AS ABAP 6.20 with certain Support Package levels.

35. Which software component allows load balancing in the context of SAP Net Weaver AS Java?

    a. SAP Web Dispatcher
    b. ABAP Dispatcher
    c. Server Process
    d. All of the above

Answer: a

Explanation:

SAP Web Dispatcher, which lies between the Internet and the SAP system, can be used as a load balancer. It is the entry point for HTTP(S) requests into your system, which consists of one or more Web application servers. As a "software Web switch", it can reject or accept connections. When it accepts a connection, it distributes the requests to ensure an even distribution across the servers (load balancing).

The SAP Web Dispatcher is a separate program that can run on a host that is directly connected to the Internet. It requires minimal configuration. You only need to enter the following data in the profile file for the SAP Web Dispatcher:

- Port on which the HTTP(S) requests are to be received (parameter icm/server_port_<xx>)
- Host and HTTP port of the SAP message server (parameter rdisp/mshost and parameter ms/http_port)

If you want to be able to call the Web application externally, for example with the URL http://shop.sap.com, this host name must be mapped internally to the SAP Web Dispatcher. This then forwards the HTTP(S) request to a suitable SAP Net Weaver AS.

36. Which of the following data sources are supported by the UME?

Note: There are three correct answers to the question

    a. Database
    b. File System
    c. ABAP User Management
    d. Directory Service
    e. Enterprise Portal

Answer: a, c, d

Explanation:

AS Java provides an open architecture supported by service providers for the storage of user and group data. The AS Java is supplied with the following service providers which are also referred to as a "user store":
- DBMS provider: storage in the system database
- UDDI provider: storage via external service providers (Universal Description, Discovery and Integration)
- UME provider: Connection of the integrated User Management Engine

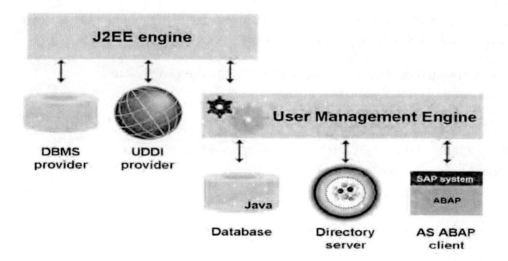

The DBMS and UDDI providers implement standards and therefore ensure that AS Java is EE-compliant. When AS Java is installed, SAP's own **User Management Engine (UME)** is always set up as the user store and is the correct choice for most SAP customers. The UME is the only way to flexibly set up and operate user and authorization concepts.

The UME supports a variety of **data sources** where user data can be stored:
- System database

- Directory service (LDAP server)
- ABAP-based SAP system (as of SAP Web AS 6.20)

37. Which of the following are the features of UME?

    a. It has its own administration console
    b. Export/Import mechanism is supported
    c. It logs important security events
    d. All of the above

Answer: d

Explanation:

Some of the important features of the UME are:

- The UME has its own administration console for administering users. It allows the administrator to perform the routine tasks of user administration, such as creating users and groups, role assignment, and other actions.
- Security settings can be used to define password policies, such as minimum password length and the number of incorrect logon attempts before a user is locked.
- The UME provides different self-service scenarios that can be used by applications. For example, a user can change his or her data, or register as a new user. Newly-created users can be approved using a workflow.
- User data can be exchanged with other (AS Java or external) systems using an export/import mechanism.
- The UME logs important security events, such as a user's successful logons or incorrect logon attempts, and changes to user data, groups, and roles.

38. Which of the following is the start sequence of components of an SAP system?

    a. Central Instance→ Central Service Instance →Database → Other Instances
    b. Central Service Instance→Central Instance→Database→Other Instances
    c. Database→Central Instance→Central Service Instance→Other Instances
    d. Database→Central Service Instance→Central Instance→Other Instances

Answer: d

Explanation:

Every SAP system has a database and at least one instance. One of these instances provides central functions and is therefore known as the central instance. The starting of the system is the task of the operating system user <system Id>adm:

The following is the sequence of steps that a SAP systems starts:

Starting the database

The database is the fundamental element of the entire SAP system. This must be is in operational state before SAP instances are created

Starting the Central Services Instances:

The central Services consist of the Java message server and the Java Enqueue server. The cluster elements like Java dispatcher and Java-server connect to the Java message server during their own start process

Starting the Central Instance

After the central services are started, the central instance is started with the java dispatcher and servers. The Java stack is started and stopped by the Java startup and Control Framework. The software deployment manager is also started with the central instance.

Other Instances

Other dialog instances are started

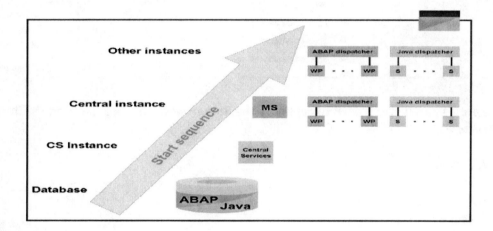

39. What is the transaction to see the Internet Communication Manager (ICM) Monitor?

    a. SM35
    b. SMICM
    c. SMQE
    d. None of the above

Answer: b

Explanation:

The Transaction SMICM is used to monitor the Internet Communication Manager (ICM). Some of the activities of ICM are stated below:

Monitoring and Restarting the ICM

Configuring the trace level and evaluating the trace files

ICM is configured using profile parameters. You can display or change these profile parameters in ICM Monitor

You can display how many requests that ICM has processed since it was started

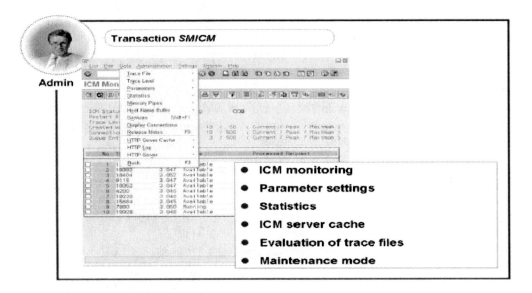

40. **What is the profile parameter is used to configure the Background work processes on the instance of the SAP system?**

    a. rdisp/btcname
    b. rdisp/vbname
    c. rdisp/wp_no_btc
    d. rdisp/vbstart

Answer: c

Explanation:

The number of work processes required in the SAP system depends on the number of tasks to be performed in the background.
Background work processes can be configured on every instance of the SAP system using the profile parameter rdisp/wp_no_btc.

41. **What is the minimum number of Background work processes are required if the transport system is used in the system?**

    a. one
    b. two
    c. three
    d. four

Answer: b

Explanation:

The number of Background work processes is required in the SAP system depends on the number of tasks to be performed in the background. If the transport system is used, there must be at least two background work processes in the system.

42. **You have two programs A and B. You need to create two jobs JOBA and JOBB to schedule the programs in background respectively. The second job JOBB should be executed only if JOBA is successful. Which option is appropriate in the Event-dependent job schedule?**

    a. After Event
    b. At Operation mode
    c. After Job
    d. Both a & b

Answer: c

Explanation:

After Job option is appropriate. You can create the job chains where the execution of the successor job can be made dependent on the status of the predecessor job.
You can see the option in the transaction SM36 as below:

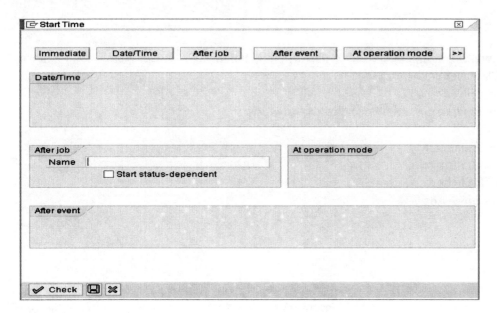

43. **What is the transaction to define Events for Background processing?**

    a. SM59
    b. SM64
    c. SM30
    d. All of the above

Answer: b

Explanation:

New Events are defined through the transaction SM64. There are two types of Events
- System Events
- User Events

You cannot modify or trigger the System Events. You can create User Events simply without tick the option "System" when creating the Event. The tick will be visible for System Events.

User Event:

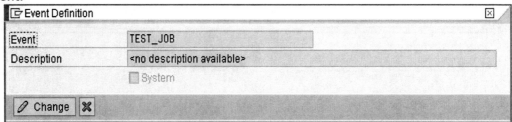

System Event:

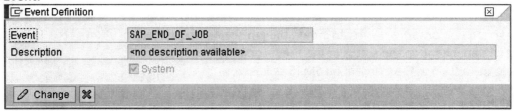

44. **Which software component is used to perform load balancing between many java instances in the context of SAP Net weaver AS Java?**

   Note: There are two correct answers to the question

   a. ABAP Dispatcher
   b. SAP Web Dispatcher
   c. Java Dispatcher
   d. Server processes

Answer: b, c

Explanation:

The SAP Web dispatcher lies between the Internet and your SAP System. It is the entry point for HTTP(s) requests into your system, which consists of one or more Web application servers. As a "software web switch", the SAP Web dispatcher can reject or accept connections. When it accepts a connection, it balances the load to ensure an even distribution across the servers.

The SAP Web Dispatcher distributes inbound requests across multiple SAP Net Weaver AS Java instances. The Java dispatcher receives the requests within an instance and distributes these to the server process of the instance.
The SAP Web Dispatcher connected in front of the multiple java Instances in the DMZ as a load balancer.

Database Administration

45. Which of the following option includes the SAP HANA's utilization of memory?

    a. Program code
    b. Program stack
    c. Memory pool
    d. All of the above

Answer: d

Explanation:

SAP HANA's utilization of memory includes its program code (exclusive and shared), the program stack and the memory pool, including all data tables (row or column), system tables and created tables. At any given time, parts of the pool are in use for temporary computations.

SAP refers to the total amount of memory in use as the SAP HANA Used Memory. This is the most precise indicator of the amount of memory that the SAP HANA database uses.

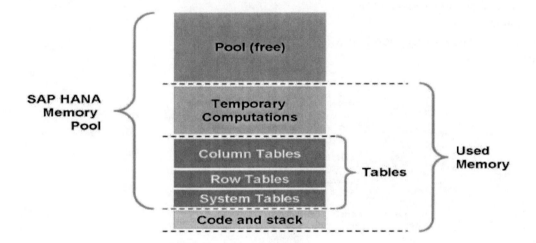

46. Which of the following events can trigger Delta merge?

    Note: There are two correct answers to the question

    a. Memory consumption of delta storage exceeds specified limit
    b. When rows and columns in a table are equal
    c. Merge is triggered explicitly by a client using SQL
    d. When memory pool is completely utilized

Answer: a, c

Explanation:

Delta merges operation:
- The delta merge operation is executed on table level.
- Its purpose is to move changes collected in write optimized delta storage into the compressed and read optimized main storage.
- Read operations always have to read from both main storage and delta storage and merge the results.
- The delta merge operation is decoupled from the execution of the transaction that performs the changes. It happens asynchronously at a later point in time.

Delta merge is triggered by one of the following events:

- Number of lines in delta storage for this table exceeds specified number
- Memory consumption of delta storage exceeds specified limit
- Merge is triggered explicitly by a client using SQL
- The delta log for a columnar table exceeds the defined limit. As the delta log in truncated only during merge operation, a merge operation needs to be performed in this case

47. **Which of the following component creates and manages sessions and connections for the database clients?**

    a. Connection and Session Management
    b. Transaction Manager
    c. Request Processing and Execution Control
    d. None of the above

Answer: a

Explanation:

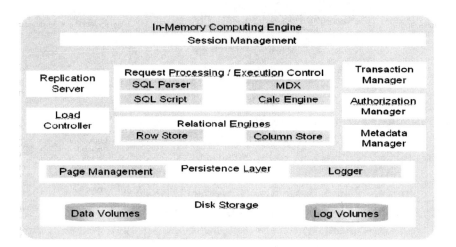

As shown in the figure above, at the top is the connection and session management which creates and manages sessions and connections for the database clients. For each session a set of parameters is maintained such as e.g. auto commit settings or the current transaction isolation level.

The client requests are analyzed and executed by the set of components summarized as Request Processing and Execution Control. Once a session is established, database clients typically use SQL statements to communicate with the in-memory computing engine.
For analytical applications the multidimensional query language MDX is supported in addition.

Features such as SQL Script, MDX and planning operations are implemented using a common infrastructure called calc engine.

At the heart of the in-memory computing engine are two relational engines. The row and the column store. These relational engines act as databases. Both are in-memory databases, that is, their primary data persistence are based in RAM.

48. **In Trigger-Based Approach which module ensures mapping between HANA DB and DB structure of source system?**

    a. Write module
    b. Read module
    c. Controller module
    d. Migration module

Answer: c

Explanation:

DB Trigger and Table-Based Delta Logging:
*   Only relevant tables considered for DB recording
*   All relevant changes are recorded in logging tables
*   Replicated changes are deleted from logging tables
*   Recording and replication possible for all table classes

Read Module:
*   Collects data changes
*   De clustering of table classes into transparent format

Controller Module:
*   Ensures mapping between HANA and DB structure of source system
*   Provides ability to conversion/migration values (e.g. date fields into strings)
*   Includes features to manage entire replication process in a holistic manner
*   Triggers activities of WRITE module

Write Module:
*   Writes data through DB connection to SAP HANA system
*   Offers flexibility to switch from single operation to array operations

49. **Which of the following factors are influenced in more complex query scenario additional CPU requirements?**

    Note: There are two correct answers to the question

    a. Data Volume

b. Query Complexity
c. I/O resource
d. User activities

Answer: a, b

Explanation:

CPU Sizing in Complex Scenarios In more complex query scenarios additional CPU requirements are influenced by the following factors:

Data volume The resource requirements for queries increase linearly with the amount of records that have to be processed.

Query complexity Queries with computationally expensive operations or complex parallelized execution plans will take more resources than the sample content queries used in the basic CPU sizing. Consequently, the CPU sizing has to be adapted accordingly.

In case that the query complexity of a customer scenario does not match or cannot be compared with the sample side-by-side scenario, throughput tests with customer specific data and queries have to be run to derive the sizing.

50. **Which of the following tasks are recommended to perform after installation?**

    a. Perform a system backup
    b. Change the passwords
    c. Finalize your customization
    d. All of the above

Answer: d

Explanation:

It is recommended to perform the following tasks after installation:

Perform a system backup: It is strongly recommended that you perform an initial backup of your system once you have finished the installation.
Change the passwords: If you are receiving a newly installed SAP HANA platform from a hardware provider, it is recommended to update the passwords so they comply with your security guidelines.
Finalize your customization: Run the SAP HANA lifecycle manager to adapt the existing configuration, if necessary.

51. **In which of the following ways a user can be created in SAP HANA database?**

    Note: There are three correct answers to the question

    a. Using CUA
    b. SAP HANA Studio

    c.   Mass user creation
    d.   SAP Net weaver Identity Management
    e.   SAP HANA Cockpit

Answer: b, d, e

Explanation:

User Administration Tools

- User management is configured using the SAP HANA studio.
- No replication of existing authorizations from source system.

By using SQL requests, for example, all the user management functions can also be executed from the command line. This is useful when using scripts for automated processing.

SAP Net Weaver Identity Management provides additional support for user provisioning in the SAP HANA database.

The SAP Net Weaver Identity Management 7.2 SP 3 contains a connector to the SAP HANA database (IDM connector). With The SAP Net Weaver Identity Management, you can perform the following actions in the SAP HANA database:

- Creating and deleting user accounts
- Assigning roles
- Setting passwords for users

The SAP HANA Web IDE contains a user editor and a catalog role editor for scenarios where only web-based tools are available.

52. A role can contain the following privileges?

    a.   System Privileges
    b.   Object Privileges
    c.   Package Privileges
    d.   All of the above

Answer: d

Explanation:

Privileges can be granted directly to users of the SAP HANA database. However, roles are the standard mechanism of granting privileges because they allow you to implement complex, reusable authorization concepts that can be modeled on business roles. Several standard roles are delivered with the SAP HANA database (for example, MODELING, MONITORING). You can use these as templates for creating your own roles.

A role can contain any number of the following privileges:

- System privileges for administrative tasks (for example, AUDIT ADMIN, BACKUP ADMIN, and CATALOG READ)
- Object privileges on database objects (for example, SELECT, INSERT, UPDATE)
- Analytic privileges on SAP HANA information models
- Package privileges on repository packages (for example, REPO.READ,
- REPO.EDIT_NATIVE_OBJECTS, REPO.ACTIVATE_NATIVE_OBJECTS)
- Application privileges for enabling access to SAP HANA XS applications

53. **If privileges are granted to a user for a package, is the user authorized for all corresponding sub-packages?**

   a. No
   b. Never
   c. Yes
   d. Sometimes

Answer: c

Explanation:

Package Privileges:
Packages contain design-time versions of various objects such as Analytic, Attribute, and Calculation Views, as well as Analytic Privileges and functions. To be able to work with packages, the respective Package Privileges must be granted.

The SAP HANA database repository is structured hierarchically with packages assigned to other packages as sub-packages.

If you grant privileges to a user for a package, the user is automatically also authorized for all corresponding sub-packages.

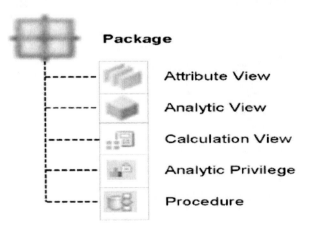

54. Which of the following packages can be edited in the system it is created?

  a. Native Packages
  b. Imported packages
  c. Attribute package
  d. Analytical Packages

Answer: a

Explanation:

The SAP HANA database repository is structured hierarchically with packages assigned to other packages as sub-packages. If you grant privileges to a user for a package, the user is automatically also authorized for all corresponding sub-packages.

In the SAP HANA repository, a distinction is made between native and imported packages. Native packages are packages that were created in the current system and should therefore be edited in the current system. Imported packages from another system should not be edited, except by newly imported updates.

An imported package should only be manually edited in exceptional cases. If you grant privileges to a user for a package, the user is automatically also authorized for all corresponding sub packages.

55. Which of the following critical system events are recorded by Audit logging?

  a. User changes
  b. Failed logons
  c. Execution of procedures
  d. All of the above

Answer: d

Explanation:

The auditing feature of the SAP HANA database allows you to monitor and record selected actions performed in your system. In other words, it provides you with visibility on who did what (or tried to do what) and when.

Audit logging records critical system events
User management: for example, user changes, role granting
System access and configuration: for example, failed logons, parameter changes
Data access: for example, read and write access to tables and views, execution of procedures
"Log all": firefighter logging, for example, for support cases

Audit policies
 • Include events to be recorded
 • If audit logging is enabled, some critical events are always logged

Audit trail

- Audit entries are created in one or more audit trails when an audit policy is triggered

56. **Which of the following different ways SAP HANA is supported for distributing data between multiple indexes servers in a single system?**

   Note: There are two correct answers to the question

   a. Index partitioning
   b. Database partitioning
   c. Table partitioning
   d. Row partitioning

Answer: b, c

Explanation:

Data Distribution: SAP HANA supports different ways of distributing data between multiple index servers in a single system:

- Different tables can be assigned to different index servers, which normally run on different hosts (database partitioning).
- A table can be split in a way that different rows of the table are stored on different index servers (table partitioning).

When a non-partitioned table is created in a distributed system, it must be assigned to one index server. By default, new tables are distributed across available index servers using a round-robin approach. For example, if there are three available index servers A, B, and C (including the master), the first table created will be located on server A, the next one on server B, the next on server C, and so on. In addition, it is also possible to specify explicitly that a table or a partition is created on a specific index server.

57. **Performance impact of using storage replication is due to following factors?**

   a. Distance between data centers
   b. Connection between data centers
   c. Latency
   d. All of the above

Answer: d

Explanation:

Storage Replication
The mirroring is offered on the storage system level. It will be offered together with the appliance as a special offering by our partners. The hardware partner will define how this concept is finally realized with his operation possibilities.

Performance impact is to be expected on data changing operations as soon as the synchronous mirroring is activated. The impact depends strongly on various external factors like distance, connection between data centers, and so on. The synchronous writing of the log with the concluding COMMITS is the crucial part here.

In case of an emergency, the primary data center is not available anymore and a process for the take-over must be initiated. So far, many customers have requested a manual process here, but an automated process can also be implemented.

This take-over process then would end the mirroring officially, will mount the disks to the already installed SAP HANA software and instances, and start up the secondary database side of the cluster. If the hostnames and instance names on both sides of the cluster are identical, no further steps with hdbrename are necessary.

58. Which of the following different replication modes available for HANA disaster recovery?

Note: There are two correct answers to the question

a. Sync
b. Half sync
c. Full sync
d. Syncdata

Answer: a, c

Explanation:

Replication Modes
When the secondary system is started in recovery mode, each service component establishes a connection with its counterpart, and requests a snapshot of the data in the primary system. From then on, all logged changes in the primary system are replicated. Whenever logs are persisted in the primary system, they are also sent to the secondary system. A transaction in the primary system is not committed until the logs are replicated.

Synchronous (replication Mode=sync)
The primary system does not commit a transaction until it receives confirmation that the log has been persisted in the secondary system. This mode guarantees immediate consistency between both systems, however, the transaction is delayed by the time it takes to transmit the data to and persist it in the secondary system.

Synchronous (replication Mode= Full Sync)
Log write is successful, when the log buffer has been written to the log volume of the primary and the secondary instance. In addition, when the secondary system is getting disconnected (e g. because of network failures), the primary systems suspends transaction processing until the connection to the secondary system is re-established. No data loss occurs in this scenario.

Synchronous in Memory (replication Mode=syncmem)

The primary system commits the transaction after it receives a reply that the log was received by the secondary system, but before it has been persisted. The transaction delay in the primary system is shorter, because it only includes the data transmission time.

Asynchronous (replication Mode=async)

The primary system sends redo log buffers asynchronously. It does not wait for confirmation from the secondary system. Secondary guarantees database consistency across all system services.
This option provides better performance because it is not necessary to wait for log I/O on the secondary system. Database consistency across all services on the secondary system is guaranteed. However, it is more vulnerable to data loss. Data changes may be lost on takeover.

59. **Which of the following options is required to protect against data loss due to disk failures?**

   a. Save points
   b. Logs
   c. Backups
   d. Memory

Answer: b

Explanation:

During normal database operation, data is automatically saved from memory to disk at regular save points. Additionally, all data changes are recorded in the redo log. The redo log is saved from memory to disk with each committed database transaction. After a power failure, the database can be restarted like any disk-based database, and it returns to its consistent state by replaying the redo log since the last save point.

While save points and log writing protect your data against power failures, save points do not help if the persistent storage itself is damaged. To protect against data loss due to disk failures, backups are required. Backups save the payload (the actual data) of the data area and log area to different locations. Currently only backups to the file system are supported.

Backups are performed while the database is running. The impact of backups on system performance is negligible, and users can continue to work normally while the backup is running.

60. **What data can be backed up and restored using backups?**

   Note: There are two correct answers to the question

   a. Data area
   b. Non-data area
   c. Log area
   d. Minute changes

Answer: a, c

Explanation:

Database should be backed up to avoid data loss due to disk failures

Database backup included back up of:
- Data area – from persistent storage to external backup locations
- Log area – is backed up automatically
- Configuration files (.ini files) – could be backed up manually

Backups save the payload (the actual data) of the data area and log area to different locations. Currently only backups to the file system are supported. Backups are performed while the database is running. The impact of backups on system performance is negligible, and users can continue to work normally while the backup is running.

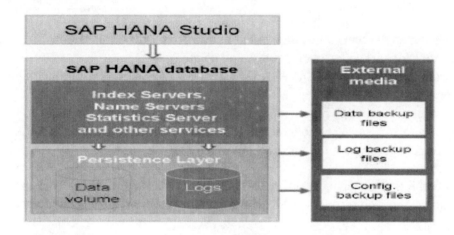

61. What are the different options for carrying out backups for SAP HANA?

a. Backups to file system
b. Backups via BACKINT interface
c. Data Snapshots using storage tools
d. All of the above

Answer: d

Explanation:

You can specify whether data and log backups are written to the file system or using third-party backup tools. The BACKINT for SAP HANA interface performs all the actions needed to write the backup data to external storage. The backup tools communicate directly with the SAP HANA database through the BACKINT for SAP HANA interface.

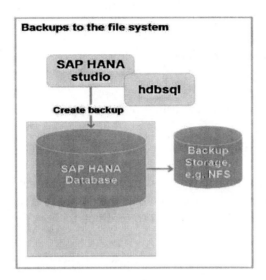
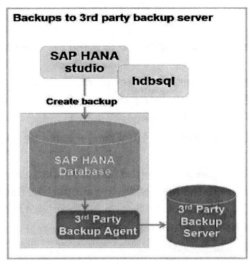

"BACKINT for SAP HANA" is an API that can be implemented by a 3rd party backup agent.
- Provides functions for backup, recovery, query, and delete.
- 3rd party backup agent runs on the SAP HANA server and communicates with the 3rd party backup server.
- Backups are transferred through pipes.
- Full integration with SAP HANA studio (configuration and execution of backups to BACKINT).
- BACKINT can be configured both for data backups and for log backups.

The default configuration is defined when a third-party backup tool is installed. After a backup tool has been installed, you can back up and recover the SAP HANA database without making any further changes.

62. **Recovering the database to a specific data backup is the only option available in the following log mode?**

   a. Normal
   b. Circular
   c. Overwrite
   d. Legacy

Answer: c

Explanation:

Overwrite mode: log_mode = overwrite
Log segments are freed by save points and no log backup is performed.
This can be useful, for example, for test installations that do not need to be backed up or recovered.

Caution: log_mode = overwrite is not recommended for production systems.
With log_mode = overwrite, no point-in-time recovery is possible. For recovery, only data backups are used; the logs are not used. Only the following recovery option can be selected: Recover the database to a specific data backup

63. Which of the following parameters makes the log area to grow until the file system is full?

    a.   When log mode is normal and automatic log backup is disabled
    b.   When log mode is overwrite and automatic log backup is enabled
    c.   When log mode is normal and automatic log backup is enabled
    d.   When log mode is overwrite and automatic log backup is disabled

Answer: a

Explanation:

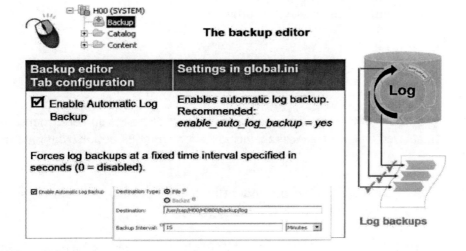

Enable_auto_log_backup: Automatic log backup can be enabled or disabled using parameter Enable_auto_log_backup.
Default: Enable_auto_log_backup = yes
Note: In the default log_mode normal, if automatic log backup is disabled, the log area grows until the file system is full. At that stage, the database will freeze.

64. How to find the memory page for a table record?

    Note: There are two correct answers to the question

    a.   A structure called "ROW ID" contains the segment and the page for the record
    b.   Secondary indexes
    c.   The page can be searched for the records based on primary key

d. The page can be searched using cluster id

Answer: a, c

Explanation:

- Each row-store table has a primary index
- Primary index maps ROW ID primary key of table
- ROW ID: a number specifying for each record its memory segment and page
- Memory page for a table record can be found:
- A structure called "ROW ID" contains the segment and the page for the record
- The page can then be searched for the records based on primary key
- ROW ID is part of the primary index of the table
- Secondary indexes can be created if needed

65. How is the Expensive Statements trace activated?

a. By entering a threshold for the statement runtime
b. By not entering a threshold for the statement runtime
c. By entering a threshold for the system runtime
d. By not entering a threshold for the system runtime

Answer: a

Explanation:

Statement Monitoring: SQL Plan Cache including execution statistics displayed on Performance tab Expensive Statements displayed on Performance tab, including configuration option (runtime threshold in micro seconds)

The SQL Plan Cache automatically collects statistics about statement execution. The runtime statistics are aggregated for all executions of the same statement.

The statistics collection can be disabled. The Expensive Statements Trace needs to be activated by entering a threshold for the statement runtime. Afterwards all statements exceeding the specified runtime are logged.

66. Which of the following system property is required to configure the system to support multitenant database containers?

a. Database isolation
b. Database Mode
c. System Usage
d. System Type

Answer: b

Explanation:

The System database of an SAP HANA multitenant database container system can be installed using the SAP HANA database lifecycle manager. Installing the System database is a prerequisite step for configuring SAP HANA multitenant database containers from the SAP HANA cockpit or the SAP HANA studio.

During installation you have to select the multiple_containers value for the *Database Mode* property to configure the system to support multitenant database containers. The *Database Mode* specifies whether the system is installed in single-container mode (default) or multiple- container mode. The system database is created during the installation process. A system administrator must create the required tenant databases after installation.

67. **Which of the following are the properties of system with high level association?**

    a. Dedicated OS user for individual tenant database
    b. Protection mechanism provided by OS
    c. Restricted access to maintain database based on roles
    d. All of the above

Answer: d

Explanation:

The properties of a system with high isolation level are as follows:

- Processes of individual tenant databases run under the dedicated OS users belonging to dedicated OS groups.

- Database-specific data on the file system is protected using OS file and directory permissions. **Note:** <sid>adm does not have OS access to tenant data volumes, log volumes, or backups, but can access tenant-specific trace and configuration files.
- Operations that require OS access are restricted to users with the correct permissions. This adds another layer of protection between tenants: tenant administrators with access to the OS cannot access other tenants or the system database using OS commands.

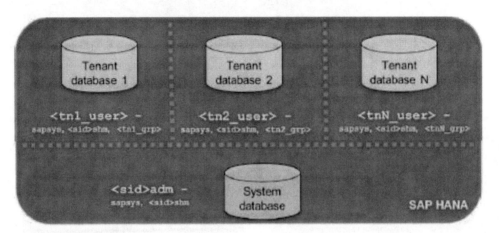

68. **Which of the following tile indicates the overall system health?**

    a. Manage Databases
    b. Manage Tenant Databases
    c. System Alerts
    d. Manage System

Answer: a

Explanation:

SAP HANA cockpit can be used to monitor the system database and any tenant database. Therefore a new catalog SAP HANA System Administration is available in the SAP HANA cockpit, which allows you to monitor and manage all tenant databases.

The following tiles are available:

Manage Databases
Indicates overall system health and provides access to the Manage Databases app where you can monitor the status and resource usage of individual databases, as well as perform other administration tasks

System Alerts
Indicates the number of high and medium alerts currently raised in tenant databases and provides access to the Alerts app where you can view and analyze alert details

69. **Which of the following component allows the web based applications to access the SAP HANA Database?**

a. Index server
b. XS server
c. Statistics server
d. Name server

Answer: b

Explanation:

The XS server allows Web-based applications to access SAP HANA via HTTP(S). The internal Web Dispatcher of the SAP HANA system manages these incoming HTTP(S) requests. To allow applications to send requests to specific databases in a multiple-container system, every tenant database needs an alias host name. Requests to the alias host name can then be forwarded to the XS server of the corresponding tenant database.

Requests with the physical host name in the HTTP host header are forwarded to the XS server running on the system database. The default HTTP ports are used in all cases, that is, 80 (HTTP) and 43 (HTTPS). Alias host names are mapped to internal HTTP(S) ports so that incoming requests can be routed to the correct database.

You configure HTTP(S) access to tenant databases by specifying in the xsengine.ini file the URLs by which each tenant database is publicly accessible. The system then automatically configures the Web Dispatcher by generating the required profile entries in the webdispatcher.ini configuration file. It is not necessary to specify the URL of the system database, this is done automatically.

Transport Management

70. **Which of the following component provides communication between the ABAP and Java stack of the Net weaver AS in both the directions?**

    a. ICM
    b. Dispatcher
    c. Message Server
    d. SAP Java Connector

Answer: d

Explanation:

- The Internet Communication Manager (ICM) is the interface to the Internet. It facilitates Web requests as a server and as a client. It supports several protocols like HTTP, HTTPS and SMTP. The SAP Net Weaver AS can be used as a web server and as a web client.

- The ABAP-Dispatcher dispatches requests to the Work Processes. If all work processes are busy at the moment the requests are placed in the Dispatcher-Queue.

- The ABAP Work Processes execute the ABAP coding.

- The Message Server exchanges messages and can perform a load balancing in the SAP system.

- The Java-side of the SAP Net Weaver AS contains components like the Java-Dispatcher (or ICM instead in some releases). Server Processes, the Software Deployment Manager (SDM) and the Central Services (SCS).

- The SAP Java Connector (JCo) provides communication between the ABAP-Stack and the Java-Stack of the SAP Net Weaver AS in both directions.

71. **Which of the following tool is used to organize, monitor and perform transports for all SAP systems within a SAP System landscape?**

    a. Transport Organizer
    b. Transport Management System
    c. R3trans
    d. All of the above

Answer: b

Explanation:

Tools of the Change and Transport System (CTS)

- The Change and Transport Organizer (CTO) provides functions for organizing software development projects. It is designed to support projects of all sizes whether they are carried out centrally or in a distributed environment.

- The Transport Management System (TMS) organizes, monitors, and performs transports for all SAP systems within an SAP system landscape. In addition use TMS to configure and manage the setting up of SAP systems and transport routes within an SAP system landscape.

- The transport tools are executables and programs that communicate with the SAP system, the database, and files generated during the transport process.

72. **Which of the following client will be used for experimenting with customization transaction and settings?**

   a. Sandbox
   b. Development
   c. Quality
   d. Training

Answer: a

Explanation:

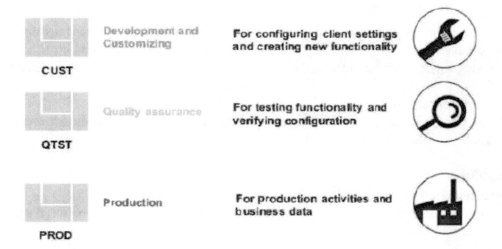

- Use the Developing and Customizing (CUST) client to configure client settings and create new functionality. CUST is the central customizing client where complete adaptation of the SAP system to customer-specific needs takes place. All changes performed in this client are recorded so they can be supplied to the other clients using the Tran sport Management System (TMS).

- Use the Quality Assurance (QTST) client for testing functionality and verifying configurations such as new customizing settings in the application.

- Use Production (PROD) client for product ion activities and business data. The PROD client is where your company's business is carried out. Customizing changes imported into this client have to be first tested carefully in the QTST client to ensure that production operation is free of disruption.

Additional Client Roles
- Use a Sandbox (SAND) client for experimenting with customizing transaction and settings.
- Use a test (TEST) client for testing configuration settings using data in a more stable environment. Customizing settings can be copied from the customizing client to the test client when performing the unit test.
- Use a Training (TRNG) client for end user training.
- Use any additional client to satisfy a customer-specific requirement.

73. **Which of the following setting for a software component helps in enhancing the object using Enhancement framework?**

    a. Modifiable
    b. Restricted Modifiability
    c. Not Modifiable; Enhanceable only
    d. Not Modifiable; Not Enhanceable only

Answer: c

Explanation:

The system change options define whether or not repository objects and cross-client customizing objects are globally modifiable. If they are globally modifiable, you can specify whether each software component and namespace can be modified in transaction SE06 Goto→System Change Option.

Software Component Settings
A software component is a set of dedicated development classes. For the software components there are four possible settings, as follows:

- Modifiable
- Restricted Modifiability (can only create objects as non-originals}
- Not Modifiable; Enhanceable Only (changes not allowed; objects can be enhanced using the Enhancement Framework only)
- Not Modifiable; Not Enhanceable (changes and enhancements not allowed)

74. **Which of the following transport routes are available in TMS?**

    Note: There are two correct answers to the question

    a. Consolidation Route
    b. Export Route
    c. Import Route
    d. Delivery Route

Answer: a, d

Explanation:

Transport routes define the flow of the transport requests from one SAP system to the next.

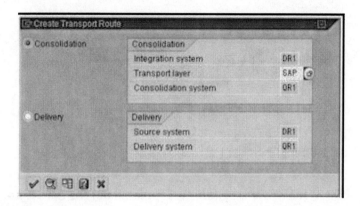

Consolidation Route
A consolidation route is an export / import route. Typically, the consolidation route proceeds from the development system (where the transport request is exported from) to the quality assurance system (where the transport requested is imported into) in a standard three system landscape. Consolidation routes have names to be addressed.

Delivery Route
A delivery route is another import route. In a standard three-system landscape the delivery route is specified between the quality assurance system and the production system because there is no additional export from the quality assurance system but another import in the production system. Delivery routes have no names.

75. Which of the following QA approval steps are available in TMS?

Note: There are three correct answers to the question

a. To be approved by department
b. To be approved by request owner
c. To be approved by System administrator
d. To be approved by Solution Manager
e. To be approved by TMSADM

Answer: a, b, c

Explanation:

When a transport request is released and exported from the development system (DEV) the import buffer of the consolidation system (QAS) is populated. The import buffer is a list of transport requests waiting for import. Once the transport request is imported into the consolidation system the import buffer for all delivery systems (PRO) is populated.

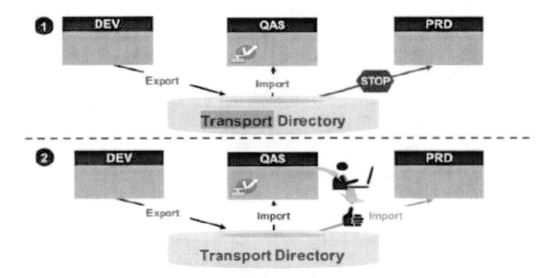

With the QA approval procedure the buffer of the delivery systems is populated but the entries are marked as inactive. In other words, the transport requests cannot be imported until the responsible person marks the transport request as approved, which results in activating the entries in the delivery systems' buffers.

TMS Quality Assurance increases the quality and the availability of the production systems by letting you check transport requests in the QA system before they are delivered to subsequent SAP systems. The SAP system for which the QA approval procedure is activated is called the QA system. When the QA approval procedure is activated a transport request will only be imported into the delivery system or systems if all the QA approval steps are processed in the QA system and the request has been approved.

76. Which of the following extended transport control scenarios can be setup in TMS?

Note: There are three correct answers to the question

    a. Client specific consolidation routes
    b. Client specific delivery routes
    c. Client specific target domains
    d. Client specific target groups
    e. Client specific domain link

Answer: a, b, d

Explanation:

Extended Transport Control Features
TMS offers the Extended Transport Control - also known as Client-specific Transport Control (CTC)-whereby the administrator can automate the process by:

- Client-specific transport target groups
- Client-specific consolidation routes
- Client-specific delivery routes

Client-specific transport targets

The transport targets of consolidation and delivery routes do not just specify an SAP system, they also specify a client. Client-specific transport targets are entered in the form: <SID>.<client> (for example, QAS .100). Transport target groups combine several client specific transport targets under a symbolic name. You can specify transport target groups when you define consolidation and delivery routes.

Client-specific consolidation routes

For each transport layer, the consolidation routes determine where changes made in the SAP system are transported to after the transport request has been released. If you have activated extended transport control, then the transport target can be a specific client in a target system or a transport target group. If you do not activate extended transport control, the transport administrator has to specify the correct target client at the time of import.

Client-specific delivery routes

Delivery routes determine whether transport requests are to be flagged for import into subsequent SAP systems/clients after they have been imported into an SAP system. If you have activated extended transport control then you can set the delivery routes as client specific. This step makes it possible to supply several clients in one AP system in sequence.

77. **Which of the following enables the customizing activities to typically create or change entries in multiple client specific tables?**

    Note: There are two correct answers to the question

    a. Table Views
    b. Table Labels
    c. Transaction STMS
    d. Transaction SM30

Answer: a, d

Explanation:

Customizing from a Technical Perspective

Customizing activities typically create or change entries in multiple client-specific tables. This step is frequently done through table views. A table view is a virtual table which presents data that is physically stored in one or multiple tables. You can compare a table view with a view that is used in an SQL database. The different customizing tables of a table view can be related to each other by foreign keys. The table entries created with the help of table views is identified by the key fields of the respective table.

In the figure customizing from a Technical Perspective the table view for maintenance Global Parameters of Countries is shown. The country parameters are maintained with the help of view V _T005. All the different attributes for a country, such as name, nationality, ISO code, date format and decimal notation are maintained. These parameters are stored physically in different tables. For example general country values in table T005, the country names in different languages in table T005T and the decimal point and date format in table T005X.

The customizer does not need to care about the technical storage of the customizing the customizer only has to maintain the information in the table view. The table maintenance can be accessed directly with the JMG or even with a generic table maintenance transaction as transaction SM30.

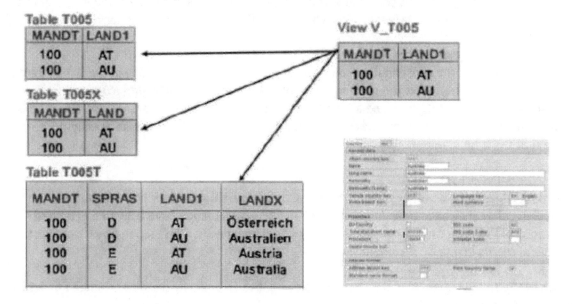

78. **Which of the following statements are true?**

    Note: There are three correct answers to the question

    a. The Project IMGs are cross client
    b. The Project IMG cannot be changed at any time
    c. All customizing activities are done directly within the project IMG
    d. A Project IMG is the Implementation Guide for a specific customizing project
    e. The project IMG are client specific

Answer: a, c, d

Explanation:

IMG Projects

Perform customizing using the SAP Implementation Guide (SAP IMG). SAP systems provide a huge variety of different business processes that can be adapted to the individual needs of a customer by customizing. An SAP ECC system contains several 10,000s of customizing tables.

The customer is guided through this customizing with the help of the IMG. An SAP system is delivered with a complete JMG for all processes available in the SAP system. This IMG is known as the SAP Reference Implementation Guide). The IMG can be accessed through transaction SPRO

The IMG provides a hierarchical list with all possible customizing activities in that SAP system. This customizing is grouped by modules and ordered in the sequence in which the individual activity has to be performed.

The IMG does not only show and group all customizing activities. The IMG also provides documentation on each customizing activity. This documentation explains the customizing activity that can be executed in this JMG node. Each customizing activity is classified into different areas.

For example, if you are interested in which customizing activity is cross-client, you can use the SAP menu: enter transaction SPRO and then choose *Additional Information→Technical Data →Client-Dependence.* There is also a classification on language dependency and on transport type that can be displayed.

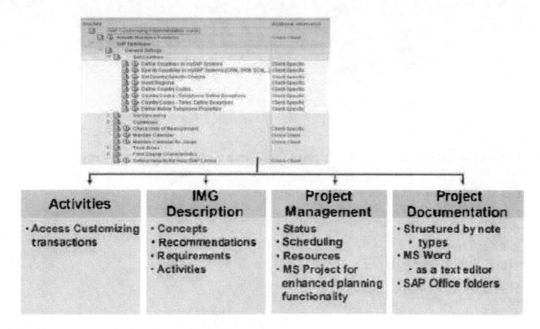

79. Which of the following information can be found in Transport Organizer?

Note: There are three correct answers to the question

a.   Transport requests for customizing
b.   Transport requests for repository objects
c.   Global transport information and status
d.   IMG Project scope
e.   Transport domain activities

Answer: a, b, c

Explanation:

The Transport Organizer is used to create, manage, release and analyze transport requests that record customizing or Repository changes. To access the Transport Organizer, you can use the transaction code SE09.

Information Provided by the Transport Organizer

- Transport requests for customizing

- Transport requests for repository objects
- Global transport information

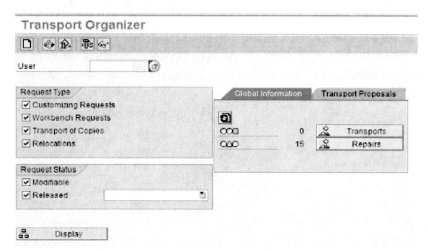

80. **Which of the following are the three basic roles found in a typical customizing project?**

   Note: There are three correct answers to the question

   a. Project Manager
   b. Customizer/Developer
   c. Operating System Manager
   d. TMS Administrator
   e. Transport configuration

Answer: a, b, d

Explanation:

Process Flow in Customizing

In an SAP implementation where customizing and development changes are integral to the SAP system being available execute projects in a structured environment using defined procedures to minimize the threat of downtime caused by program or business configuration errors.

The goal of your project organization is to divide the large number of activities among the project team so the team members do not interfere with each other's work. Make sure that work logically belongs together but is being performed by different team members. This process is carried out by dividing the tasks in a customizing project among three roles each of which is responsible for performing certain tasks.

Project Manager
The project manager creates the transport requests and assigns the appropriate members to them. When a member is assigned to a transport request the SAP system creates a task; the settings for each member are recorded in his or her task. For the transport to other SAP systems the project manager can release the created transport requests.

Customizer /Developer

Customizers perform their customizing using the IMG and the developers perform their development mainly using the ABAP Workbench tools. They assign their work to their individual tasks in the transport requests assigned to them. For client-specific data the customizers can copy their settings to the *TEST* client to test them. Both customizers and developers are authorized to release their own tasks in a transport request but are not allowed to release the transport request.

TMS Administrator

The TMS administrator uses the TM S to transport released transport requests to subsequent SAP systems in the SAP system landscape using the predefined paths.

81. **What recommendations does change management for development include?**

    Note: There are three correct answers to the question

    a. Restrict Repository Object changes
    b. Define development standards
    c. Define Customizing transport request
    d. Use projects to group transport requests
    e. Reinitialize the TMS configuration for every transport request

Answer: a, b, d

Explanation:

Recommendations for development change management include the following:

- Perform development efforts in a single environment only: the development system where you set the system change options.
- Use packages to group functionally-related repository objects. The transport layer assigned when creating a package enables the same predefined transport route to be used for all objects in the package.
- When releasing a transport request document the purpose and the status of the changes.
- To maintain security use authorizations to control which users can create, modify, or release transport requests. SAP delivers sample authorization profiles that provide the SAP system access required for various levels of responsibility in change management.

Most customers have to define development rules, customizing rules and transport rules. These rules describe how and where changes are made, how and where these changes are tested, how the quality assurance is done and how and who creates, releases and imports transport requests in the SAP system landscape.

82. **Which of the following are the attributes of repository objects?**

    Note: There are two correct answers to the question

    a. Package
    b. Version

  c. Person Responsible
  d. Original Language

Answer: c, d

Explanation:

Attributes for Repository Objects

The attributes for repository objects include the following:
- Package
- Person responsible
- Original system
- Original language

Attributes for each repository object are assigned by the SAP system. The object directory is stored in table *TADIR.* This table is central to your SAP system's consistency. To change entries in *TADIR* use only the standard functions SAP provides.

With the appropriate authorization you can modify the package and person responsible for the object. To modify object directory entries from the Workbench Organizer call transaction SE09 and choose Goto →*Transport Organizer Tools*. Alternatively, use transaction SE03.

Some repository objects may be generated automatically by the SAP system as a result of customizing activities. In the object directory, these SAP system created objects are identified as "generated".

83. Which of the following statements about SSCR registration are true?

 Note: There are two correct answers to the question

  a. All users must register with SSCR
  b. A User who uses the ABAP workbench to create, modify or delete repository objects must register with SSCR
  c. All SAP Repository objects that will be modified must register with SSCR
  d. Only customer objects are required to be registered with SSCR

Answer: b, c

Explanation:

Any user in an SAP system who wishes to use the ABAP Workbench to create, modify, or delete repository objects, including customer objects must be registered using the SAP SSCR process. Such users are referred to as development users or developers.

Registration can be done at SAP Service Marketplace http: //service.sap.com/sscr. As a result of the registration process, each developer is assigned an access key. The access key is entered and saved on the developer's SAP system in the table DEV ACCESS.

The access key is associated with the developer's logon ID and the SAP system's license number. The developer is prompted for the access key during the initial attempt to create or change a repository object.

You register developers and all SAP Repository objects (not customer objects) that are to be modified. When registering an object you supply the object program ID object type, object name, the SAP system's license number, and the release of your SAP system. After registering an SAP object in an SAP system and applying the access key, the key is stored in the database table ADIRACCESS. This step will ensure that further changes to the object do not require another key. Registered object keys become invalid after a release upgrade.

SSCR provides development reliability, rapid error correct ion and high system availability. This step can be done by limiting the access to the development and object keys. Most customers are doing the registration of objects and developers centrally.

84. **Which of the following are the different types of transport request classifications?**

   Note: There are three correct answers to the question

   a. Object
   b. Package
   c. Unclassified
   d. Local
   e. Transportable

Answer: c, d, e

Explanation:

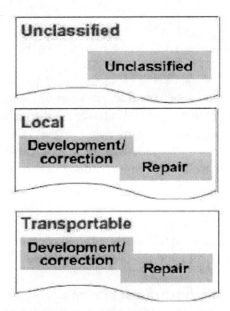

A distinction is made between two types of development tasks: development/correction (considered one task) or repair. Development/correction is a change in the original system, and repair is a change in an SAP system other than the original system.

Objects saved as local objects cannot be transported. The only way to transport such an object is to assign it to another package, one that has an existing transport layer assigned.

The package of the repository object determines whether the transport request type is transportable or local. If the assigned package has a valid transport layer a transportable request is used. Otherwise, a local transport request is used.

Characteristics of Transport Requests
- Transport requests or tasks of type Unclassified have empty object lists.
- Changes to original objects are saved to tasks of type Development/correction.
- Changes to copies are saved to tasks of type Repair.
- The package of a repository object determines when a transport request of Transportable or Local is required.

85. **When a transport request is released which of the following subdirectories does the system update at the file system level?**

    Note: There are three correct answers to the question

    a. Buffer
    b. Queue
    c. Co files
    d. Control Files
    e. Data

Answer: a, c, e

Explanation:

The first step in the transport process is to release a transport request and export all the associated objects from the database of the development system (DEV) to files in the common transport directory at file system level. For each transport request released the data is exported to a data file in the subdirectory data and a control file is written to the subdirectory co files. During the export the entries required for the subsequent import are created in the import buffers of the target systems and a test import can be performed.

In the directory buffer at file system level is an import buffer file for each SAP system in the transport domain. The file is named after the corresponding SAP system ID and contains control information regarding the transport requests to be imported and the order of import.

Several transport control commands can be used to manage the import buffer files at the operating system level. The control information in the import buffer files is read and represented in import queues accessed from within the SAP system. An import queue shows all transport requests that are listed in the corresponding buffer.

86. Which of the following statements about importing into a production system are true?

Note: There are three correct answers to the question

a. Production system should be shutdown
b. No user should be working with the affected business processes
c. No batch jobs running related to the affected business processes
d. No RFC communication related to the affected business processes
e. Change the role of production client to allow modifications

Answer: b, c, d

Explanation:

Requirements for Importing into PRD
The system you work on may determine what you can do. While importing into QAS requires no ongoing testing related to the affected business processes importing into PRD requires the following:

- No users working with the affected business processes
- No batch jobs running related to the affected business processes
- No RFC communication related to the affected business processes

After export, a request is not automatically imported but must be manually imported. When planning imports include enough time to accommodate post -import tasks such as the quality assurance testing we recommend planning imports at regular intervals such as monthly.

87. Which of the following import options are supported in TMS?

Note: There are two correct answers to the question

a. Select requests according to filter settings
b. Complete projects
c. All transport requests in the QA work list
d. All transport request in the PROD work list

Answer: a, b

Explanation:

Importing and Marking Objects for Import

The objects from the transport requests marked for import will be imported as follows:
- All objects of all selected transport requests are merged together.
- First of all the objects are sorted according their level (such as table definitions before programs).
- In the case of an object in more than one transport request only the version in the last transport request is imported (according to the sequence in the import queue).

System Monitoring (AS ABAP and AS Java)

88. Which of the following actions is possible using the Monitor Browser in NWA?

Note: There are two correct answers to the question

a. Changes to threshold values
b. Delete History values
c. Cross system monitoring
d. Display Monitoring data for Java Instances

Answer: a, d

Explanation:

Monitoring Browser
The tasks of the Monitor Browser are to change threshold values, and display collected monitoring data. The monitoring browser is available in the NWA. The monitoring browser shows the current status of the monitoring attributes and you can maintain thresholds and activate/deactivate monitoring attributes.

89. Data in the monitoring infrastructure is grouped into the following areas?

a. Kernel
b. Application
c. Services
d. All of the above

Answer: d

Explanation:

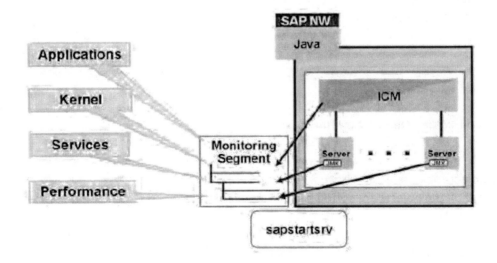

The data in the monitoring infrastructure is grouped in several areas like Kernel, Services, Performance and Applications.

- **Kernel:** Status information for the managers registered for monitoring is displayed under the Kernel entry.
- **Performance:** The Performance area displays available data about performance measurements of the SAP Net Weaver AS Java, e.g. communication to external systems.
- **Services:** Status information for the services registered for monitoring is displayed under the Services entry.
- **Applications:** This branch contains information about the status of applications that are running on the SAP Net Weaver AS Java and for which monitoring functions are implemented in the coding. This is a configurable type of monitor, since you can specify which information is displayed in the monitor for your own applications. An application developer usually creates his or her own monitors and objects under the *Applications* branch. The other monitor branches, such as Kernel, System, and so on are reserved for data that is directly and automatically collected by the system.

90. **Which of the following monitoring tool helps to monitor multiple SAP systems and their operating systems?**

    a. RZ20
    b. SAP MMC
    c. System Overview
    d. Monitoring Browser

Answer: a

Explanation:

RZ20: The RZ20 in a CEN (central monitoring system with) is a powerful tool to monitor multiple SAP systems and their operating systems. You can set up additional notifications in case of alerts and auto-reaction methods there.

Beyond that, you are able to view the current status and open alerts of monitoring attributes. You can maintain thresholds and complete open alerts.

The RZ20 gets her information out of the monitoring segment of the AS Java, this means, that e.g. performance issues of the AS Java doesn't affect the monitoring and alerting in the CEN system.

91. **Which of the following agents are used to deliver the runtime monitoring of the AS Java data to the Central Monitoring system?**

    Note: There are two correct answers to the question

    a. Host agent
    b. CCMS agent
    c. Instance agent
    d. Monitoring agent

Answer: a, c

Explanation:

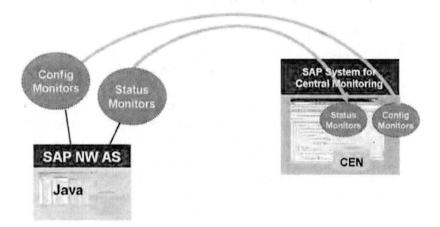

If the SAP Net Weaver AS Java starts, JMX monitors are created. They deliver data for runtime monitoring. To deliver the data to the CEN the SAP Net Weaver management agents are used.

The SAP Net Weaver management agents are used to administer and monitor SAP Net Weaver components. They are automatically installed and started during the installation of any SAP Net Weaver components as of release SAP EHP2 for SAP Net Weaver 7.0 (in short 7.02) or SAP Net Weaver 7.1.

There are two types of agents, depending on the associated component: the **host agent** and the **instance agent**. One host agent runs for each monitored host (including hosts on which one or more instance agent is running). An instance agent runs for each monitored instance.

92. **In which of the following monitor status of the monitoring data is stored?**

   Note: There are two correct answers to the question

   a. Engine
   b. Application
   c. Interface
   d. Service

Answer: a, b

Explanation:

You can display the J2EE monitoring data in the central monitoring system using the Alert Monitor. To do this, you must open the Alert Monitor (transaction RZ20 in client 000) and select the monitor set SAP J2EE Monitor Templates. The status data is stored in the following monitors:

- The Engines monitor displays status data for the kernel, services, performance, and the system.
- The Applications monitor displays application data.

In the SAP Net Weaver AS Java status monitors, you can see at a glance where warnings (yellow) and errors (red) have occurred. If you open the tree at the corresponding places, you learn more about the cause.

93. **Which of the following different scenarios exist for setting up GRMG monitoring?**

    Note: There are two correct answers to the question

    a. Technical Customization of GRMG application
    b. GRMG Monitoring settings adjustment
    c. Instrument the application for GRMG Monitoring
    d. GRMG infrastructure using XML format

Answer: a, c

Explanation:

The following different scenarios exist for setting up GRMG monitoring:

Technical Customizing for monitoring a GRMG application

You have a complete Java application with a built-in GRMG application (from SAP or programmed yourself) and want to activate the availability monitoring for Java/HTTP-compatible components or Java applications.

Note: This process is suitable for consultants and customers who want to activate GRMG monitoring for an application that is already instrumented for monitoring with the GRMG.

Instrument the application for GRMG monitoring

You have a Java component or applications for which you want to create GRMG monitoring. You need to store all of the information (host name, application, and so on) required for an automatic GRMG request in a GRMG Customizing file. Create the messages that are to be returned in the GRMG response and create a monitor definition in the CCMS Alert Monitor.

Note: This process is primarily suitable for application developers working for customers or partners who want to equip their own components for GRMG monitoring.

94. **Which of the following monitor definitions are offered by CCMS?**

    Note: There are two correct answers to the question

    a. Rule Based Monitors
    b. Static Monitors
    c. Statistical Monitors
    d. Self Repairing Monitors

Answer: a, b

Explanation:

SAP delivers preconfigured monitor sets that you can use immediately. Each monitor set bundles monitor definitions that display various parts of the entire monitoring architecture, by topic area. It is therefore easier, for example, to access monitoring data referring to the database (for example).

"Monitor definition"
A **monitor definition** describes the selection of monitoring objects and monitoring attributes you would like to look at. Monitor definitions are bundled to monitor collections in transaction RZ20. If you double-click a monitor definition, the referred data will be collected and the corresponding monitor will be displayed.

Monitor
A **monitor** is the graphical representation of all monitoring objects and monitoring attributes that should be displayed according to the monitor definition.

95. **With which of the following transactions you can activate a trace for SQL statements in the SAP System?**

    Note: There are two correct answers to the question

    a. Performance Trace
    b. System Log
    c. System Trace
    d. Database Performance Analysis

Answer: a, c

Explanation:

- You can analyze SQL statements by activating the trace in transaction ST01 (System Trace) or ST05 (Performance Trace).
- Transaction SM21 (System Log) is the system log
- ST04 (Database Performance Analysis) is used to analyze database statistics.

96. **Which of the following software components needs to be implemented to use the end to end monitoring and alerting infrastructure function?**

    a. Wily Intro scope agent
    b. SMD Agent
    c. SAP Host Agent
    d. All of the above

Answer: d

Explanation:

Remote systems are also named managed systems or satellite systems. SAP Solution Manager is sometimes labeled as managing system.

To be able to use the end-to-end monitoring and alerting infrastructure (MAI) function. Fundamentally, you need to implement the following software components:

Wily Intro scope Agents (or IS Agents)

This remote component collects Performance data and metrics from different technical components and comes in different forms. For example the Wily Intro scope Byte code Agent This collects performance data and metrics out of a Java Server process. The collected information is transferred to the Wily Intro scope Enterprise Manager.

Wily Intro scope Enterprise Manager (EM)

This serves as a central repository where all information collected by Wily Intro scope Agent performance data and metrics are stored centrally.

Solution Manager Diagnostics Agent (or SMD-Agent)

The Solution Manager Diagnostics Agent (or SMD agent) allows a connection between SAP Solution Manager and the managed system to produce and to collect information from the remote system. It must be installed once per host or virtual host.

SAP Host Agent

SAP host agent is the component that monitors the host / operating system interaction. It will be installed once per physical host, which should be monitored.

97. **Which of the following saves the data to a product instance perspective with an Info Cube?**

    a. EFWK
    b. ST-PI
    c. ST-A/PI
    d. None of the above

Answer: a

Explanation:

EFWK

The Extractor Framework (EFWK) processes the information of the connected ABAP systems and the Wily Intro scope Enterprise Managers within the SAP Solution Manager. The EFWK saves the data to a product instance perspective within an Info Cube. The Info Cube is a technical object and a component of the Net Weaver Business Intelligence (BI).

ST-PI and ST-A/PI

An Interface for the collection and transmission of data and performance metrics of ABAP components (technical they are two SAP software components). The Extractor Framework (EFWF) fetches the data into the SAP Solution Manager system.

98. **Which of the following function displays the development of the most important metrics of your managed objects?**

a. Alert Inbox
b. Interactive Reporting
c. Generated Documents
d. All of the above

Answer: b

Explanation:

The functions available within this work center are accordance with the functional areas in the configuration section with the following exceptions:

Alert Inbox - Is the central access point for analyzing and solving Technical Monitoring problems in an SAP Solution Manager landscape

Interactive Reporting - Displays the development of the most important metrics of your managed objects (like systems, hosts and databases), centrally, to identify potential problems early, and give an overview of the load, availability and performance of these objects. The life time and granularity was defined during configuration of the system monitoring scenario.

Generated Documents – Allows you to access Early Watch Alert Reports (EWA), Early Watch Alert for Solution Reports (EWA fS) and Service Level Report (SLR) which are available within the SAP Solution Manager

99. **What is the prerequisite for the usage of administration or configuration tools of SAP Net Weaver AS Java?**

a. The database must be running
b. Instance must be created
c. Control services must be activated
d. None of the above

Answer: a

Explanation:

There are four administration or configuration tools are available for SAP Net Weaver AS Java. They are:
- Config Tool
- SAP Net Weaver Administrator
- Visual Administrator
- Shell Console Administrator

All the above tools are required a primary prerequisite is the Database must be running
During the start process of the SAP Net Weaver AS Java instance, the parameters for the start and running operation are read from the database and copied to the file system. These parameters are maintained in the database. It is therefore, the database should be running before configuring these tools.

100. **Which component of SAP Net Weaver Development Infrastructure (SAP NWDI) is used to structure the transport landscape in the context of SAP Net Weaver AS java?**

a. Design and Time Repository (DTR)
b. Component Build Service (CBS)
c. Change Management Service (CMS)
d. None of the above

Answer: c

Explanation:

The Change Management Service (CMS) domain contains the transport directory with which transports of your software changes can be handled.
You create a domain using the CMS Web interface in the browser with the URL
http://<CMS-Host>:<port>/devinf and go to the area change management service→ Landscape configurator.

101. **Which statements are true in the context of Transporting Java objects?**

Note: There are two correct answers to the question

a. When importing requests into the consolidation system, the activation of objects is usually started automatically
b. As in the ABAP environment, only individual development objects are imported into the production system
c. During the assembly step, only links to required software components are created
d. All required software components are included in the archive to be created during the assembly step

Answer: a, c

Explanation:

Unlike the central development system, where the activation must be explicitly started by the developer, the activation is automatically started during the import into the consolidation system. In contrast to the ABAP environment, the entire software components are delivered in an archive file and imported.

During the assembly step, only links to required software components are generated. These software components themselves are not included in the archive. If however the required software components are not available in a successor system, an error message appears when you attempt to import.

102. **Which type of transport request will be created for ABAP Programs?**

a. Customizing Transport Request
b. Workbench Transport Request
c. Both a & b

d. None of the above

Answer: b

Explanation:

When you create a ABAP program, a workbench transport request is created. ABAP programs are client independent objects.
Customizing Transport Requests will be created for all customizations having the client dependent objects.

103. **Which user is created automatically when you include an SAP system in the transport domain in the transaction STMS?**

a. SAPJSF
b. SAPUSR
c. TMSADM
d. None of the above

Answer: c

Explanation:

When you include an SAP system in the transport domain in the STMS, the system performs the following actions automatically:
*   Creates the user TMSADM
*   Generates the RFC destinations required for the TMS
*   Sends the address data to the domain controller
*   Sends the profile parameter for configuring the transport control program to the domain controller
*   Configures the SAP System as a single system

104. **Which table contains the object information of the transport request?**

a. E070
b. E071
c. SE11
d. None of the above

Answer: b

Explanation:

*   E071 is the table that contains the object details of the transport request. You can get a transport request and their objects inside.
*   E070 is the table that contains only transport requests and their descriptions.
*   SE11 is used for ABAP dictionary.

105.   Which of the following are the tree parts of the CCMS Alert monitoring Infrastructure?

a. Data collection
b. Data storage
c. Administration
d. All of the above

Answer: d

Explanation:

The CCMS alert monitoring infrastructure consists of three parts:
- Data Collection
- Data storage
- Administration

At the data collection level, small areas of an SAP system are monitored by special programs called data collectors. Data collectors can be ABAP, C or JAVA programs. Each Data collector checks its subcomponent at regular intervals and stores the collected monitoring data in the main memory

At the data storage level, the area of the main memory that contains the monitoring data from the data collector is called the monitoring segment. The data collection and storage elements must be present on every component that is to be centrally monitored.

The administration level allows the data from monitoring segment to be displayed and evaluated.

106.   If an SAP system with software component SAP_BASIS has 4 instances, how many monitoring segments can exist?

a. 4
b. 8
c. 6
d. 2

Answer: a

Explanation:

Note that every instance of an SAP system with software component SAP_BASIS has its own monitoring segment in the shared memory. The number of instances determines the number of monitoring segments whether or not several instances running on the same hardware is of no significance.
There will be 4 monitoring segments for the SAP system having 4 instances.

107.   Which of the following transaction is used to configure SAP Connect?

a. SCAT
b. SCC1
c. SE38

d. SCOT

Answer: d

Explanation:

The Transaction SCOT is used to configure the SAP connect. You can set up communication types here (such as fax, internet, email...etc) by creating and configuring communication nodes. You can use various views of the communication infrastructure in transaction SCOT.

The following steps to perform to send messages using communication type in the transaction SCOT:

- You have to activate the communication type
- You require at least one communication node for the communication type
- All programs that may be required must be available and configured

108. **Which of the following are the primary settings required to run eCATT scripts in a landscape consisting of multiple systems?**

   a. RFC connection between the systems involved
   b. Creating a System data container
   c. Both a & b
   d. None of the above

Answer: c

Explanation:

If your company wants to implement an AS ABAP as the central system for eCATT to be able to run it in a landscape consisting of multiple systems, you should primary configure the below settings

- **RFC connections between the systems involved**
You must configure the RFC connections between central systems to the systems tested. You can create the RFC connections using the RFC destinations using the transactions SM59. SAP recommends setup trusted RFC connections in this context. The use of trusted RFC is that Remote Function call can be performed in the target system without the need to transfer a password.

- **Creating a system data container**
A system data container stores the system landscape for test scenario. It contains a list of all systems that a test script can access. Every entry in this list describes a system and consists of:
   - A name for the target system
   - A description of the relevant software component purely for documentation purpose
   - An RFC connection that points to target system

109. **Which local monitoring service is used to debug the J2EE applications?**

   a. SQL Trace

b. Single Activity Trace (SAT)
c. System Trace
d. Application Trace

Answer: d

Explanation:

The application trace service is a profiling tool for developers for debugging J2EE applications during runtime. A fast trace is often required, without setting up the VM in debug mode, restarting the container, or redeploying the application. The application trace is integrated into the Visual Administrator as a service.

Application Tracing Service aims to provide application developers with a high-level, powerful tool for on-the-fly debugging of J2EE applications. The necessity of a quick trace without having to set up the Virtual Machine (VM) in debug mode, restart the container, or redeploy the application is frequently proven.

Byte code modification is used as the basis for application tracing. When an application is set up in "byte code-modified" mode, it is restarted and its new class loader knows that there are changes to be made in the byte codes. Once debugging is over, the application can be started again in normal mode. The old classes and class loaders will be garbage-collected.

The profile-based settings of the Application Tracing Service are stored on the server and are persistent. They can be used to tune the balance between optimizing speed and memory, as well as to select the level of complexity of the data that is displayed.

You can use this service to trace your applications without having to do any programming yourself. The runtime control provides you with everything you need for proper application tracing.

110. **Which CCMS agent is used to transfer the data from JMX monitors to the central monitoring system?**

a. SAPCCMSR
b. SAPCCM4X
c. SAPCM3X
d. None of the above

Answer: a

Explanation:

The SAPCCMSR.INI configuration file is stored in the working directory of the CCMS agent. The name of the file is always SAPCCMSR.INI, irrespective of the agent type. It primarily contains path specifications that are required for the operation of the CCMS agents

The functional principle of the CCMS agent SAPCCMSR has been extended in case SAPCCMSR is monitoring a J2EE Engine. In a case of this type, it must be possible that the monitoring segment of the

SAPCCMSR agent does not belong to the central monitoring system. This is achieved by extending the system term to include Java components (such as J2EE Cluster). The SAPCCMSR agent with the -j2ee option exists for this purpose.

111.   Which of the following steps required for installing the SAPCCMSR agent?

   a. Create the CSMREG user in the central monitoring system
   b. Create the CSMCONF file in the central monitoring system
   c. Register the agent in the Visual Administrator
   d. All of the above

Answer: d

Explanation:

The installation of SAPCCMSR agent requires all the three steps. They are:
   • Create the CSMREG user in the central monitoring system
   • Create the CSMCONF file in the central monitoring system
   • Register the agent in the Visual Administrator

The CSMREG user is used for communication between the SAPCCMSR agent and central monitoring system. This user is a communication user with very specific authorizations. The administration user is only used to create the RFC connection from the agent to the central monitoring system.

The agent requires a file called   CSMCONF. It is stored in the SAPCCMSR agent working directory /usr/sap/ccms/<SID_Instance>/sapccmsr. This file contains users and important system information for central monitoring system. It contains the entries about the CSMREG user and an administration user. The SAPCCMSR agent should be registered in the Visual Administrator.

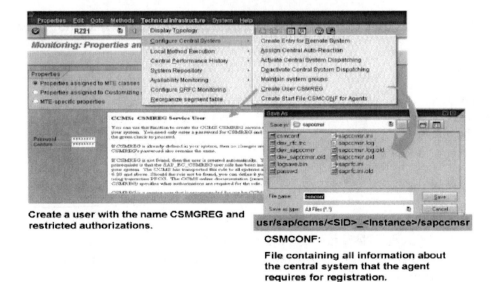

Create a user with the name CSMGREG and restricted authorizations.

usr/sap/ccms/<SID>_<Instance>/sapccmsr

CSMCONF:

File containing all information about the central system that the agent requires for registration.

112.   **Which of the following transactions are used to display the profile parameters?**

Note: There are two correct answers to the question

a.   RZ11
b.   RZ20
c.   RSPFPAR
d.   RZ15

Answer: a, c

Explanation:

The current values of the profile parameters can be displayed in the system. There are two ways to do it.
- Transaction RSPFPAR
- Transaction RZ11

Both functions display the profile parameters for the instance in which the user is currently logged on. The transaction RSPFPAR displays the list of all instance-specific profile parameters which is updated with the system-wide parameters.

The transaction RZ11 displays the information and documentation for individual profile parameters. It also shows whether the parameter can be changed while the system is running with the Dynamically Switchable indicator.

113.   **What is the sequence of steps that you perform to setting up the operation modes?**

a.   Create Operation modes => Distribute Work Processes => Maintain Time table => Assign Instances
b.   Create Operation modes => Maintain Time table => Distribute Work Processes => Assign Instances
c.   Create Operation modes => Assign Instances => Distribute Work Processes => Maintain Time table
d.   Distribute Work Processes => Maintain Time table => Create Operation modes => Assign Instances

Answer: c

Explanation:

Steps to configure the Operation Modes as below:

- Operation Modes are created as empty containers in transaction RZ04
- All active instances of the system are detected and the work processes defined in the instance profile are assigned to the operation modes as default values
- You can now make allocations for the individual operation modes in the total number of work processes taken from the instance profile.

- You then specify the periods for which the operation modes are valid and when the switch between the operation modes should occur in the time table (SM63)

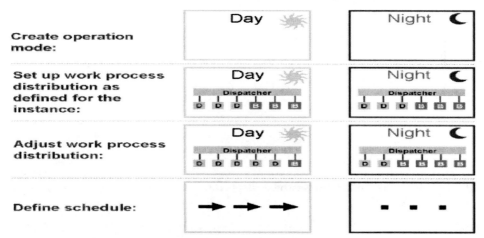

114. **When Central User Administration (CUA) is activated, what are the configurations are performed automatically in the system?**

   a. The corresponding ALE model is created or adjusted
   b. Partner Profiles are created
   c. Text comparison with the child system is carried out for roles
   d. All of the above

Answer: d

Explanation:

When the CUA is activated, the system carries out the following configuration steps automatically:
The corresponding ALE model is created or adjusted to match the new CUA model if changes have been made
The ALE distribution model defines which applications communicate with each other in the distributed systems and which data types are distributed.
Partner Profiles are created
Partner profiles define the conditions for electronic data exchange via the IDOC interface.
Text comparison with the child systems is carried out for roles (and profiles)
The check tables and the texts for roles, profiles, and license data in the individual child systems are saved temporarily in the central system

115. **What is the report used to delete the Central User Administration completely?**

   a. RSDELAUTH
   b. RSDELCUA
   c. RSDELTXI
   d. None of the above

Answer: b

Explanation:

You can remove Central User Administration (CUA) again, simply by performing the reverse of the set up first in the central system and then in all child systems. The first three steps (transactions SCUG, SCUM, and SCUA) are combined in the report **RSDELCUA**. You then cancel settings in transactions WE20 and BD64, and if necessary also in transaction SM59.

Procedure in the Central System
- Log on to the central system.
- Run report RSDELCUA (Using transaction SE38).
- The system displays the screen Delete Entire Central User Administration. The name of the distribution model is displayed under Central User Administration.
- In the Delete section, choose the Complete CUA, and set the Test indicator. Then choose *Execute*. The system displays an overview of the data to be deleted. You can jump to transaction SE16 by double clicking.
- If you are happy with the test result, choose back and deselect the test indicator. Then choose *Execute*. The system displays an overview of the deleted data.
- In transaction WE20, delete the data about the sending system (central system) and the receiving systems (child systems)
- In the Implementation Guide (IMG, transaction SALE), choose Modelling and Implementing Business Processes Maintain Distribution Model and Distribution Views (transaction BD64).
  - In change mode, select the model (in this example, CUA), and choose Delete
  - Choose Save

Procedure in Child System

- Delete the data for the sending system (central system) in transaction WE20.
- In the Implementation Guide (IMG, transaction SALE), choose Modelling and Implementing Business Processes Maintain Distribution Model and Distribution Views (transaction BD64).
- In change mode, select the model (in this example, CUA), and choose Delete.

The users of the child system remain as users in the CUA and are globally locked there. This means that these users can never be completely deleted. If you recreate CUA and want to include the child system in CUA again, you must perform a user transfer again.

116.   **Which prerequisites must be fulfilled on the SAP side to connect an AS ABAP with a directory server?**

   Note: There are two correct answers to the question

   a. Host name and Port number of the directory server are maintained under connection data
   b. In user maintenance, there is a user of type system that has read and writes authorization for the directory server
   c. The operating system program *ldap_rfc* runs on the same host as the directory server
   d. The names of the RFC destination and the associated connector definition are identical

Answer: a, d

Explanation:

In the SAP system, The RFC destination used and the LDAP connector must be maintained with the same name (in uppercase letters). The operating system program *ldap_rfc* can then be started on the selected application server of the SAP system while the directory servers addressed can run on remote servers.

Additional customizing settings include the definition of a system user and the connection data. As well as the host name and port number of the directory server.

The LDAP system user is stored in customizing for the directory service connection and has nothing to do with the SAP users maintained in transaction SU01.

117.   **Which of the following are the types of data distributed during the ALE distribution model defined for the Central User Administration (CUA)?**

Note: There are two correct answers to the question

a.   Company addresses
b.   Sales Organizations
c.   User master data
d.   Material master data

Answer: a, c

Explanation:

The ALE distribution model defines which applications communicate with each other in the distributed systems and which data types are distributed. You require a separate ALE distribution model for a Central user Administration.

In the central system, you define the structure of your Central User Administration in the model view, which you then distribute to the child systems.

There are two types of data are distributed in this context. They are:
- User Master data (Including assigned roles and profiles)
- Company addresses

In the distribution model, you require two methods to distribute user data and company addresses. To implement these methods, you use BAPIs of the USER and USERCOMPANY business objects with the CLONE method.

SAP System Concepts

118.   Which of the following are the tasks of an RFC interface?

Note: There are three correct answers to the question

a.   Handles errors
b.   Data Conversion
c.   Communicate between systems
d.   Assigns the authorization objects in remote system
e.   Communicates with the Java based systems

Answer: a, b, c

Explanation:

RFC is an SAP interface protocol that is based on the Common Programming Interface for Communication (CPI-C) and allows cross-host communication between programs. This enables external applications to call ABAP functions and SAP systems to contact (RFC-enabled) external applications.

RFC means that ABAP programmers do not have to write their own communication routines. For an RFC call, the RFC interface

- Converts all parameter data to the format required in the remote system
- Calls the communication routines that are required to communicate with the remote system
- Handles errors that occur during the communication

The RFC interface is easy for the ABAP programmer to use. The processing steps for calling external programs are integrated into the CALL FUNCTION statement.

119.   What is the access method is used on UNIX based systems in the context of Local Printing?

a.   Access Method S
b.   Access Method U
c.   Access Method C
d.   Access Method L

Answer: d

Explanation:

Use local printing if the host spool system (operating system spooler) and the spool work process of the SAP System are on the same host.
Local printing is the fastest and most reliable form of printing from the point of view of SAP Systems.

You can use local printing for the following operating systems:

- Microsoft Windows
- UNIX

When you are configuring the output device in a device definition, you specify how the printer is connected to the SAP System using the access method.

The access method specifies whether you are using local or remote printing. The access method is identified by a letter and informs the system which architecture is in use and which operating system you are using. In this way, the system knows the way in which data is to be transferred.

The following Access methods are used:

Access method **C**: Microsoft Windows
Access method **L**: UNIX

120.   **You are running a small company having 60 employees. You want to run the SAP in your company which covers the core processes such as Finance and Sales. Which SAP product is recommended to implement in your company?**

  a.   SAP Business Suite
  b.   SAP Business All-in-one
  c.   SAP Business One
  d.   None of the above

Answer: c

Explanation:

SAP Business One is an integrated ERP solution developed specially for small and mid-sized companies. This is the ideal solution for small companies with less than 100 employees and 30 users who are looking for an affordable system that covers their core processes. The remaining SAP products are developed for midsized and above companies.

121.   **Which of the following statements are true for tRFC?**

  Note: There are three correct answers to the question

  a.   The two systems involved must be accessible at the time of the call
  b.   Genuine Asynchronous communication Method
  c.   The Remote system does not have to be available at the time of call
  d.   It is used if a function is to be executed as a Logical Unit of Work (LUW)
  e.   tRFC doesn't require any system resources

Answer: b, c, d

Explanation:

Transactional RFC (tRFC) is an asynchronous communication method that executes the called function module just once in the RFC server. The remote system need not be available at the time when the RFC client program is executing a tRFC. The tRFC component stores the called RFC function, together with the corresponding data, in the SAP database under a unique transaction ID (TID).

If a call is sent, and the receiving system is down, the call remains in the local queue. The calling dialog program can proceed without waiting to see whether the remote call was successful. If the receiving system does not become active within a certain amount of time, the call is scheduled to run in batch. tRFC is always used if a function is executed as a Logical Unit of Work (LUW).

122.   Which of the following RFC variant can you use to process work steps in parallel?

a.   Synchronous RFC
b.   Asynchronous RFC
c.   Both a & b
d.   None of the above

Answer: b

Explanation:

Parallel-processing is implemented with a special variant of asynchonous RFC. It's important that you use only the correct variant for your own parallel processing applications: the CALL FUNCTION STARTING NEW TASK DESTINATION IN GROUP keyword.

123.   Which of the following is the successor to transactional RFC?

a.   sRFC
b.   aRFC
c.   bgRFC
d.   tRFC

Answer: c

Explanation:

Synchronous RFC (sRFC)
For direct communication between different systems and between SAP Net Weaver AS and SAP GUI
Asynchronous RFC (aRFC)
For direct communication between different systems and for parallel processing of selected tasks
Transactional RFC (tRFC)
For genuine asynchronous communication Transactional RFC ensures "transaction-like" processing of processing steps that were originally autonomous.
Queue (d) RFC (qRFC)
Queued RFC is an extension of tRFC. It also ensures that individual steps are processed in sequence.
Background RFC (bgRFC)
bgRFC is the successor to tRFC and qRFC. The use of bgRFC instead of tRFC and qRFC is urgently recommended.

bgRFC is the successor to tRFC and qRFC, with significant improvements in terms of performance and functional capability. Consequently, SAP urgently recommends using bgRFC instead of tRFC and qRFC.

124.   SAP Support packages will be used for the following purpose?

Note: There are two correct answers to the question

    a. To keep the SAP System at the latest maintenance level
    b. To enter user data
    c. To implement adjustments in SAP system due to changes in legal requirements
    d. To import all transport requests that SAP makes available in SAP Service Marketplace

Answer: a, c

Explanation:

SAP Support Packages are not used to enter user data. Customer developments are transported to other SAP systems using transport requests. Transport requests from SAP are imported with the Transport Management System (TMS).

SAP Support Packages are bundles of repository objects and customizing. In principle, each software component and each release level has its own SAP Support Packages. In the case of software components that intersect (with modified add-ons, for example), there is an additional type of SAP Support Package, the Conflict Resolution Transport (CRT). Technically speaking, SAP Support Packages are a kind of transport request that cannot be imported as a normal transport request, however.

A SAP Support Package contains all known, relevant SAP Notes that have been created since the last SAP Support Package for the corresponding software component - and additional objects, that were not delivered by an SAP Note. It can also contain new customizing and customizing that has been corrected since the last SAP Support Package.

SAP Support Packages are not cumulative, but are based on their predecessors. In principle, importing SAP Support Packages for one particular software component is independent of the level of SAP Support Packages of other software components. The individual components are in general independent of one another. However, there can be cases where the importing of individual SAP Support Packages leads to side-effects. Importing an SAP_HR SAP Support Package can require the previous import of a SAP_BASIS SAP Support Package, or an SAP_APPL SAP Support Package, for example. As soon as they have been identified, these side-effects are documented in a composite SAP Note that is referenced when importing SAP Support Packages.

125.   What can be done with the maintenance transaction?

Note: There are two correct answers to the question

    a. Import support packages
    b. Calculate support packages stacks of your SAP system
    c. Approve objects in your download basket
    d. Import SAP Notes and Enhancement Packages

Answer: b, c

Explanation:

A maintenance transaction cannot import SAP Notes, Support Packages and SAP enhancement packages. SAP Notes are imported via the Note Assistant, Support Packages for AS ABAP based systems via transaction SPAM, and Support Packages for AS Java based systems via tool *JSPM*, SAP enhancement packages via the tool *SAPehpi*.

126.   **Which of the following status indicates maintenance certificate is nonexistent in Change Management Work Center?**

   a. Red
   b. Yellow
   c. Green
   d. Grey

Answer: a

Explanation:

Status check of maintenance certificates in the connected systems

To see the status of the managed systems in SAP Solution Manager you open the transaction SM_WORKCENTER there. Navigate to the *Change Management* work center. Here you can view the status of all connected systems with respect to a valid contract, licenses and maintenance certificates.

Within the field Status of automatic distribution can be inferred that the automatic distribution is enabled for this system. This usually happens automatically when the SAP system is connected to the SAP Solution Manager (transaction SOLMAN_SETUP). If this is not the case, the automatic distribution will be activated with the push button automatic distribution.

If the field maintenance validity has a red status, this means that this system do not have a valid contract at SAP. The fields for the connected system have the following meaning:

Status	License	Maintenance certificate
Red	Valid to have been exceeded.	Valid to have been exceeded. A system check has rated the maintenance Certificate as nonexistent
Yellow	Valid to will be reached in less than 30 days.	Valid to will be reached in less than 30 days. A system check would still rate the maintenance certificate as existing.
Green	License is valid.	Maintenance certificate is installed and valid
Gray	No data. Rating is not possible.	No data. Rating is not possible.

127. **SPAM/SAINT update can be performed in which of the following situation?**

    a. SAP system having aborted support packages
    b. SAP system have no aborted support packages
    c. SAP system have over written support packages
    d. SAP system have error prone support packages

Answer: b

Explanation:

The SPAM/SAINT update is imported using the transaction SPAM. You can only import a SPAM/SAINT update if there are no aborted SAP Support Packages in the SAP system. If there are aborted SAP Support Packages, a dialog box informs you of this. You then have two options:

- You first import the complete queue of SAP Support Packages and then the SPAM/SAINT update.
- You reset the status of the queue, import the SPAM/SAINT update first and then the SAP Support Package queue. You can reset the status of the queue by choosing *Extras → Reset status → Queue.*

128. **What is the transaction to import support packages?**

    a. SNOTE
    b. SPAM
    c. SU21
    d. None of the above

Answer: b

Explanation:

The transaction SPAM (Support Package Manager) provides you with an easy and effective way of importing SAP Support Packages into your system.
Support Packages are available in SAP Support Portal, under service.sap.com/patches or on collection CDs.
Support Package Manager runs at the SAP system level. Knowledge of the operating system is therefore not required for handling this tool.
The Support Package Manager update is shipped in English and German only. If you are working in any other language, new or updated user interface elements or texts might be displayed in English or German only. We therefore recommend that you logon in either English or German when using Support Package Manager.

129. **Which of the following statement is true regarding the transaction SPDD Adjustments?**

    Note: There are two correct answers to the question

Answer: a, d

Explanation:

The SPDD adjustments should be performed manually in each system of the landscape but not to be imported to the subsequent systems with transport requests. Importing transport requests leads to inconsistency in the Repository objects.

- The SPDD transaction adjusts only Dictionary repository objects.
- The SPDD adjustments should be performed manually in each system of the landscape
- The SPDD adjustments can be imported to each system of the landscape by transport orders
- The SPDD transaction adjusts non-Dictionary Repository objects
- The SPDD transaction adjusts Dictionary Repository objects

130.   **In which of the following situation SUM tool can be used for applying support packages?**

Note: There are two correct answers to the question

a. Very less number of support packages to apply
b. Very huge number of support packages to apply
c. In downtime critical situation
d. Resource optimization situation

Answer: b, c

Explanation:

The steps to start the SUM are as follows:

1. Copy the SUM package to the host of the SAP system, for example into the *sapmnt\SYS\<SID>* directory
2. Extract the SUM package - which will result in around 3500 files
3. Start the SUM controller by starting a startup script from the SUM root directory
4. Connect via a browser to *http://<host name>:4239* - now the SUM start page and the SUM front end start
5. Log on to the SUM front end

The same as with SPAM, these steps would be performed first on the development system, then on the quality assurance system, then on the productive system.

Note: For SUM for AS ABAP based SAP systems, a stack.xml file - created by Maintenance Optimizer - is mandatory to apply SAP Support Packages!

As a conclusion you can say: use SPAM in normal cases, use SUM if you have to apply a huge number of SAP Support Packages in a very downtime critical SAP system.

SPAM/SAINT	SUM
Easy handling	Short Downtime
Test mode, showing modification preview	Shows point of no return with reset option
Check for SAP Notes currently more precise	Checks available disk free space and database free space
Does not require SAP Solution Manager for MOpz	Uses Stack.xml for valid setup
Can work with Third Party Add-ons unknown to MOpz	Runs separately, outside SAP system
	Can restart the SAP system, and switch the kernel

131. **In which of the following module, objects of support packages are inactively imported in downtime minimized mode?**

   a. Preparation
   b. Import 1
   c. Import 2
   d. Clean Up

Answer: b

Explanation:

The four modules execute the following steps:

Preparation module: All the preparatory steps and check steps (such as the test import, add-on conflict check) are performed in this module. The module can run during production operation. Once the preparation module has been completed, you still have the option of resetting or deleting the queue. If you continue with the Import 1 module, data is changed on the database and the queue can no longer be reset or deleted.

Import 1 module: In this module, the objects of the SAP Support Packages are imported. If the import procedure is carried out in **Downtime-minimized** mode, programs are inactively imported. The runtime system cannot "see" these changes yet. Dictionary objects are inactive when imported, independent of the import mode. The manual modification adjustment of the Dictionary objects is performed at the end of this module, if required (SPDD modification adjustment). If you can guarantee that no manual changes are required for the SAP system and no transports are imported into the SAP system during this time, up to here this module can run during production operation.

Import 2 module: Now the dictionary objects are activated. The remaining import steps are carried out in this module. If you use the **Downtime-minimized** import mode, inactive programs are activated in this module as well. During this module **production operation is not permitted** to avoid inconsistencies and data loss. As a result, this module always means SAP system **downtime**.

Clean Up module: In this module, all the clean-up steps are processed. The modification adjustment of the non-Dictionary repository objects is performed in this module (SPAU modification adjustment). When all modifications have been adjusted, production operation can continue.

132. **Which of the following are the advantages of SAP Enhancement packages?**

    a. Simple adaptation to legal requirements
    b. Easier to maintain and plan
    c. New functionality can be activated as and when required
    d. All of the above

Answer: d

Explanation:

SAP enhancement packages are therefore an upgrade of individual software components with the advantage that the new functions can be activated when required.

Note: Selective activation of business functions of an SAP enhancement package is only possible in certain AS ABAP-based SAP systems!

The advantages of SAP enhancement packages are:
- Simple adaptation to legal requirements
- Easier to maintain and plan
- Fewer complete SAP system upgrades necessary
- The new function can be activated as and when required (only possible in some AS ABAP-based SAP systems)

Note: An SAP enhancement package not only delivers software components of an SAP system, but also different SAP systems of an application, for example SAP ERP.

As such, SAP Enhancement Package 6 for SAP ERP 6.0 contains some software components of an SAP ECC 6.06 system, and additional software components or content of an SAP Net Weaver Portal 7.03 system, and components of an SAP XSS 606 system. An SAP enhancement package can therefore include elements for various components in an application.

133. **Which work processes are used to administer the lock table in the shared memory?**

    a. Dialog work Processes
    b. Update work Processes
    c. Enqueue work processes
    d. Background work processes

Answer: c

Explanation:

Work processes execute the individual dialog steps in R/3 applications. The various work processes are:

Dialog Work Process

Dialog work processes deal with requests from an active user to execute dialog steps.

Update Work Process

Update work processes execute database update requests. Update requests are part of an SAP LUW that bundle the database operations resulting from the dialog in a database LUW for processing in the background.

Background Work Process

Background work processes process programs that can be executed without user interaction (background jobs).

Enqueue Work Process

The Enqueue work process administers a lock table in the shared memory area. The lock table contains the logical database locks for the R/3 System and is an important part of the SAP LUW concept. In an R/3 System, you may only have one lock table. You may therefore also only have one application server with Enqueue work processes.

Spool Work Process

The spool work process passes sequential datasets to a printer or to optical archiving. Each application server may contain only one spool work process.

The services offered by an application server are determined by the types of its work processes. One application server may, of course, have more than one function. For example, it may be both a dialog server and the Enqueue server, if it has several dialog work processes and an Enqueue work process.

User Administration (AS ABAP and AS Java)

134. In AS ABAP system user requests are processed by?

a. Dispatcher
b. Web service
c. OS processes
d. SAP Work process

Answer: d

Explanation:

The term **user** usually means user ID here.
People log on to an operating system, a database, or an SAP system using a user/password combination
Operating systems, databases, and SAP systems usually have different authorization concepts. If a user/password combination is created in an SAP system for a person, this does not mean that it is possible to log on to the operating system of a host with the same user/password combination. However, it is possible that identical user/password combinations are created for SAP systems and operating systems.

Note: User requests are processed by SAP work processes. These work processes all use a common user to access the database.

135. Which of the following objects requires protection in SAP system?

a. Customer Master Record
b. Lock Entries
c. Company codes
d. All of the above

Answer: d

Explanation:

Access to the operating system level of the application server and database server must be protected, otherwise it may not be possible to use the SAP systems or the data could become damaged.

A person can log on to a client of an SAP system if he or she knows the user name and password of a user master record, and if the user type is authorized for the log-on type. For example, it is not possible to log on with a communication or system user in the **dialog process**.

In the SAP system, there is an authorization check every time a transaction is called. If a user attempts to start a transaction for which he or she is not authorized, the system rejects the user with an appropriate error message.

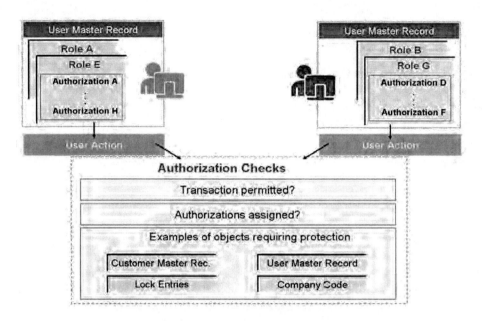

136. **User authorizations are assigned using the following?**

Note: There are two correct answers to the question

a.   Authorization Objects
b.   Roles
c.   Profiles
d.   Field values

Answer: b, c

Explanation:

If the user starts a transaction for which he or she has authorization, the system displays the initial screen of this transaction. Depending on the transaction called, the user enters data and performs actions on this screen. There may be additional authorization checks for the data and actions to be protected.

User authorizations are assigned using roles (and sometimes through *manual* profiles, for example SAP_NEW). The authorizations are combined in roles and the roles are entered in the user master record.

137. **Which of the following user types is not SAP GUI capable?**

Note: There are two correct answers to the question

a.   Dialog
b.   Communication
c.   System
d.   Service

Answer: b, c

Explanation:

System
Use the *System* user type for dialog-free communication within a system or for background processing within a system, or also for RFC users for various applications, such as ALE, Workflow, Transport Management System, and Central User Administration. It is not possible to use this type of user for a dialog logon. Users of this type are excepted from the usual settings for the validity period of a password. Only user administrators can change the password.

Communications Data
Use the *Communications Data* user type for dialog-free communication between systems. It is not possible to use this type of user for a dialog logon. The usual settings for the validity period of a password apply to users of this type.

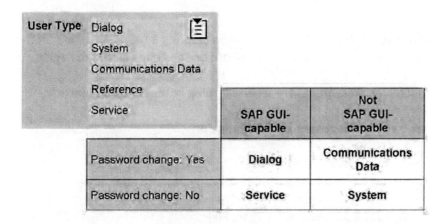

138.   **Which of the following input fields are mandatory for creating a user master record?**

        Note: There are three correct answers to the question

a.   Last Name
b.   Initial Password
c.   Repeat Password
d.   Personalization
e.   Default printer

Answer: a, b, c

Explanation:

Creating a new user master record
To start user maintenance (transaction SU01), choose *Tools → Administration → User Maintenance → Users* in the SAP menu [S000].

You can create a new user master record by copying an existing user master record or creating a completely new one. The user master record contains all data and settings that are required to log on to a client of the SAP system. This data is divided into the following tab pages:

- **Address:** Address data
- **Logon data:** Password and validity period of the user, and user type.
- **SNC:** stands for Secure Network Communications, and is used for security functions (external product) that are not directly available, but have been prepared in SAP systems.
- **Defaults:** Default values for a default printer, the logon language, and so on.
- **Parameters:** User-specific values for standard fields in SAP systems.
- **Roles and profiles:** Roles and profiles that are assigned to the user.
- **Groups:** For the grouping of users for mass maintenance.
- **Personalization:** In some transactions, personal settings are required which have some affect on the appearance. These can be stored (prepopulated) using personalization objects.
- **License Data:** On this tab page, you specify the contractual user type of the user Evaluation in the system measurement.

You must maintain at least the following input fields when creating a user: Last name on the *Address* tab page, initial password and identical repetition of password on the *Logon Data* tab page.

139.   Which of the following statements are true regarding authorization objects?

Note: There are two correct answers to the question

a.   Authorization objects allows complex checks
b.   An authorization is always associated with exactly one authorization object
c.   Authorization objects cannot be customized as per customer requirement
d.   Authorization objects contain only one Activity Field

Answer: a, b

Explanation:

In an ABAP-based SAP system, actions and access to data are protected by authorization objects. The authorization objects are delivered by SAP and are in SAP systems. To provide a better overview, authorization objects are divided into various object classes.

Authorization objects allow complex checks that involve multiple conditions that allow a user to perform an action. The conditions are specified in authorization fields for the authorization objects and are AND linked for the check.

Authorization objects and their fields have descriptive and technical names. In the example in the figure, the authorization object User master maintenance: User Groups (technical name: S_USER_GRP) contains the two fields "Activity" (technical name: ACTVT) and "User Group in User Master Record" (technical name: CLASS). The authorization object S_USER_GRP protects the user master record. An authorization object can include up to ten authorization fields.

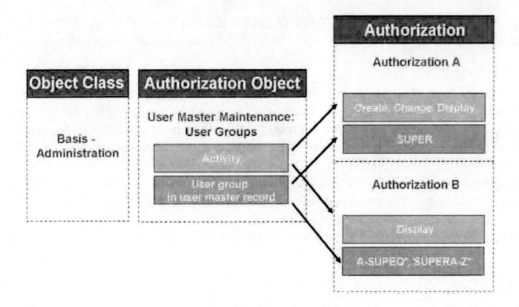

An authorization is always associated with exactly one authorization object and contains the value for the fields for the authorization object. An authorization is a permission to perform a certain action in the SAP system. The action is defined on the basis of the values for the individual fields of an authorization object.

For example: Authorization B in the graphic for the authorization object *S_USER_GRP* allows the display of all user master records that are not assigned to the user group *SUPER*. Authorization A, however, allows records for this user group to be displayed.

There can be multiple authorizations for one authorization object. Some authorizations are delivered by SAP, but the majority is created specifically for the customer's requirements.

140.   **SAP Authorization concept is a positive concept because of the following?**

   a.   Every user automatically receives all authorizations
   b.   Authorizations must be explicitly assigned
   c.   The range of features of the authorization check is so large
   d.   The developers programmed it efficiently

Answer: b

Explanation:

When the user calls a transaction, the system checks whether the user has an authorization in the user context that allows him or her to call the selected transaction. Authorization checks use the authorizations in the user context. If you assign new authorizations to the user, it may be necessary for this user to log on to the SAP system again to be able to use these new authorizations.

If the authorization check for calling a transaction was successful, the system displays the initial screen of the transaction. Depending on the transaction, the user can create data or select actions. When the user completes his or her dialog step, the data is sent to the dispatcher, which passes it to a dialog work process for processing. Authority checks (*AUTHORITY-CHECK*) that are checked during runtime in the work process are built into the coding by the ABAP developers for data and actions that are to be protected.

If the user context contains all required authorizations for the checks (return code = 0), the data and actions are processed, and the next screen is displayed. If one authorization is missing, the data and actions are not processed and the user receives a message that his or her authorizations are insufficient. This is controlled by the evaluation of the return code. In this case, it is not equal to 0.

All authorizations are permissions. There are no authorizations for prohibiting. Everything that is not explicitly allowed is forbidden. This can be considered as a "positive authorization concept".

141.   Which of the following is used to maintain the roles in SAP system?

    a.   Transaction PFCG
    b.   Profile Generator
    c.   Activity Groups
    d.   All of the above

Answer: d

Explanation:

Role Maintenance (transaction PFCG, previously also called Profile Generator or activity groups) simplifies the creation of authorizations and their assignment to users.

In role maintenance, transactions that belong together from the company's point of view are selected. Role maintenance creates authorizations with the required field values for the authorization objects that are checked in the selected transactions.

A role can be assigned to various users. Changes to a role therefore have an effect on multiple users. Users can be assigned various roles.

The user menu comprises the role menu(s) and contains the entries (transactions, URLs, reports, and so on) that are assigned to the user through the roles.

142.   Suppose an Employee X works in ABC company and meets Employee Y who works in PQR Company. They discuss some internal issues of ABC Company. Which of the following threat X pose to ABC Company?

    a.   Spoofing
    b.   Code Injection
    c.   Social Engineering
    d.   Authorization misuse

Answer: c

Explanation:

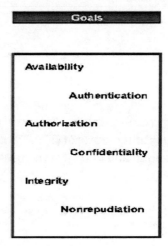

The threats shown in the figure are only a set of commonly known threats. A major security threat is social engineering where sensitive information is exposed casually or picked up without going through the correct channels.

Case Study - Social Engineering Threats
The case study is a good example which shows the proper procedures that should be maintained for a secure environment.

A security consultant was asked to visit a large company and evaluate the security lapses in the company. The man with whom the consultant was supposed to work was quite busy and left the consultant alone saying he would be back soon. After an hour the consultant walked down to the computer room but could not get in because it was a secure room. When another employee arrived and swiped his own access card, the consultant was let into the computer room.

While inside the secure room the consultant saw a note card next to the terminal with the administrator password written on it; he logged on to the server.

The consultant worked on the computer for about 45 minutes. Then, an employee said that he and his coworkers were going out to lunch. The consultant was left alone in the computer room for another hour.

The security consultant finished his work and returned to the desk of the man with whom he was supposed to work. The man was apologetic and asked the consultant to return the next day. The security consultant replied that he was already finished working and that the company had numerous security lapses.

143.   Which of the following is a process to modify the Internet Protocol address of the source of the Transmission Control Protocol / Internet Protocol (TCP/IP) packet?

    a.   SQL Injection
    b.   Cross Site Scripting
    c.   Spoofing

d.   Message Flooding

Answer: c

Explanation:

Spoofing
Programs can be written to modify the Internet Protocol (IP) address of the source of the Transmission Control Protocol/Internet Protocol (TCP/IP) packet and trick the network because the true IP identity is concealed or disguised and looks like the packet is coming from within the network. This process is known as spoofing.

144.   **Which of the following are the service providers in an open architecture of Application server Java (AS Java)?**

Note: There are three correct answers to the question

a.   DBMS Provider
b.   Access Control List
c.   UDDI Provider
d.   UME Provider
e.   ABAP Engine Provider

Answer: a, c, d

Explanation:

AS Java provides an open architecture supported by service providers for the storage of user and group data.
The AS Java is supplied with the following service providers (user store):

- **Database Management System (DBMS) provider:** This is used for storage in the system database.
- **Universal Description, Discovery and Integration (UDDI) provider**: This is used for storage using external service providers.
- **UME provider:** This is used to provide connection of the integrated UME.

The DBMS and UDDI providers implement standards and therefore, ensure that AS Java is Java 2 Enterprise Edition (J2EE)-compliant. When AS Java is installed, SAP's own UME is always set up as the user store and is the preferred choice for most SAP customers. The UM E is the only way to flexibly set up and operate user and authorization concepts.

145.   **Which of the following are the functions of the User Management Engine (UME) parameter?**

Note: There are two correct answers to the question

a.   Data Source
b.   Mobile Notification
c.   Email Notification

d.   Administrative Policy

Answer: a, c

Explanation:

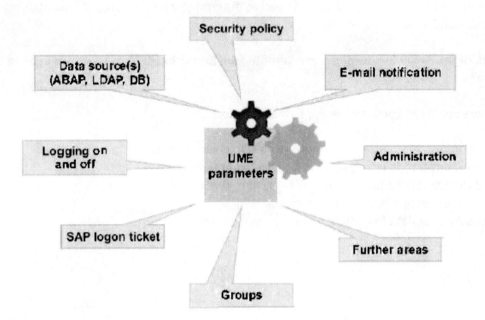

After you have selected and configured a data source, there are many other parameters with which you can influence the behavior of the UME. The figure provides an overview of the relevant Areas.

The important UME parameters are as follows:

- Date source(s)
- Security policy
- E-mail notification
- Logging on and off
- SAP logon ticket
- Groups
- Administration

146.   **Which of the following are the key benefits of Central User Administration (CUA)?**

   Note: There are two correct answers to the question

a.   You can maintain roles in one place
b.   You can reduce the cost of user administration
c.   You can create user data from multiple places
d.   You can provide secure user administration by centralizing the work

Answer: b, d

Explanation:

Central User Administration (CUA)
The aim of CUA is to reduce the cost of user administration and to make user administration more secure by centralizing the work. CUA envisions only a single client for maintaining user data. Therefore to administer user data using CUA, you need to determine where you will be maintaining your users in your system landscape.

147.   **For which of the following purposes are Remote Function Calls (RFC) connections used in the CUA scenario?**

   Note: There are three correct answers to the question

   a.   To distribute user data from the central system to child systems
   b.   To distribute user data from one child system to another
   c.   To send changes to the data in the central systems to the child systems
   d.   To send status reports back to the central system
   e.   To distribute user data from child system to central system

Answer: a, c, d

Explanation:

RFC Connections

RFC connections are used to exchange data by ALE in the context of CUA. RFC connections are used to distribute user data from the central system to child systems, to send changes to this data in the child systems and to send status reports back to the central system.

In the context of CUA, the central system is treated like another child system in some respects. In the simplest case of CUA (two logical systems linked to each other, one central system and one child system, within the same SAP system), two RFC connections are required. If the central system and child system are in different SAP systems, three RFC connections are required.

The RFC connections required are as follows:

- RFC connections from the central system to itself (loopback)
- RFC connections from the central system to the child systems
- RFC connections from the child systems to the central system

148.   **Which component of the SAP Governance, Risk and Compliance (GRC) solution provides the ability to manage and monitor user privileges?**

   a.   Risk Management
   b.   SAP Access Control
   c.   SAP Process Control
   d.   Global Trade Services

Answer: a

Explanation:

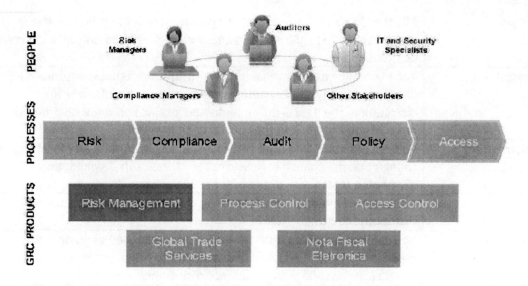

The Access Risk Management process provides the ability to manage and monitor user privileges while ensuring compliance with security policies related to SoD and restriction of critical permissions. You can prevent, monitor, and manage access conflicts present at the system, infrastructure and application levels.

149.   If you are using **Central User Administration**, you can use the distribution parameters in the transaction SCUM to determine where individual fields of a user master record are maintained. Which parameter setting is recommended for the fields that contain the data maintained by the users themselves?

a. Global
b. Proposal
c. Redistribution
d. Both a & b

Answer: c

Explanation:

For each field of transaction SU01, you can use the transaction SCUM to determine the system in which the administration of the field content can be performed.

The following parameters available in the transaction SCUM to determine the fields of user master records:

Global	You can only maintain the data in the central system. The data is then automatically distributed to the child systems. These fields do not accept input in the child systems, but can only be displayed. All other fields that are not set to "global" accept input both in the central and in the child systems and are differentiated only by a different distribution after you have saved.
Proposal	You maintain a default value in the central system that is automatically distributed to the child systems when a user is created. After the distribution, the data is only maintained locally, and is not distributed again, if you change it in the central or child system.
Redistribution	You can maintain data both centrally and locally. After every local change to the data, the change is redistributed to the central system and distributed from there to the other child systems.
Local	You can only maintain the data in the child system. Changes are not distributed to other systems.
Everywhere	You can maintain data both centrally and locally. However, only changes made in the central system are distributed to other systems, local changes in the child systems are not distributed.

150.   **What is the authorization object for system assignment in Central User Administration?**

    a.   S_USER_SAS
    b.   S_USER_AGR
    c.   S_USER_PRO
    d.   S_USER_SYS

Answer: d

Explanation:

All user administrators of a CUA system group can exist in the central CUA, but each user can assign authorizations only for one part of the connected systems.
You can distribute users from a central system to various child systems of a system group. The object S_USER_SYS is used to check the systems to which the user administrator can assign the users.

Special Authorization Objects for CUA

Authorization Object	Meaning
S_USER_SYS	System assignment in CUA
S_USER_SAS	Role and profile assignment to systems in CUA

CPSIA information can be obtained
at www.ICGtesting.com
Printed in the USA
LVOW09s2038041217
558599LV00030B/751/P